A GOURMET GUIDE TO
Oil and Vinegar

A GOURMET GUIDE TO

Oil and Vinegar

DISCOVER & EXPLORE THE WORLD'S
FINEST SPECIALITY SEASONINGS

URSULA FERRIGNO

Photography by JAN BALDWIN

RYLAND PETERS & SMALL
LONDON • NEW YORK

*For Antonia, my little girl,
whose passion for oil started
at one-and-a-half and has
continued to surprise me.*

ISBN: 978-1-84975-575-7

A CIP record for this book is available
from the British Library.

US Library of Congress cataloguing-in-
publication data has been applied for.

Printed and bound in China

Note
• All eggs are medium (UK) or large (US)
unless otherwise specified

Senior designer Toni Kay

Commissioning editor Nathan Joyce

Production controller David Hearn

Art director Leslie Harrington

Editorial director Julia Charles

Picture research Christina Borsi

Prop stylist Jo Harris

Food stylist Emma Marsden

Indexer Diana Le Core

First published in 2014 by
Ryland Peters & Small
20–21 Jockey's Fields, London
WC1R 4BW
and
Ryland Peters & Small Inc.
519 Broadway, 5th Floor
New York, NY10012

www.rylandpeters.com

10 9 8 7 6 5 4 3 2 1

Text © Ursula Ferrigno 2014
Design and photographs
© Ryland Peters & Small 2014

Contents

Introduction

When I announced to my family and friends that I was writing a book about oil and vinegar, I was surprised by their reaction, which was generally either 'is there enough to write about?' or 'aren't they just for salad dressings?'. Oh how wrong can they be!

I have to say that oil in particular is the most absorbing and tantalising of subjects, as well as being exotic and romantic, because its origins are shrouded in mystery. Every oil producer I have met is truly passionate about this noble fruit and their determination and dedication to produce and perfect this historic food is remarkable. I have found the subject matter utterly fascinating and also rather humbling, as I feel like there is so much to learn.

Some of my earliest memories in Italy are of my grandfather showing me precisely how to taste oil. I enjoyed watching him smack his lips enthusiastically and closing his eyes if the oil he was trying was good! Good oil is bountiful in the lands surrounding the Mediterranean Sea and many have access to excellent oil, which is often stored in large cans, carboys or demijohns and decanted into smaller vessels as needed. La dispensa (the store cupboard) is incomplete without these magical dark bottles filled with oil for the coming months.

The opportunity to smell and taste great oil and vinegar as a child has stayed with me to this day. I think that there's nothing in the world that compares with a good, freshly milled oil. If you love something, you tend to want to proclaim it as far and wide as possible, and through this book, I hope that's what I've achieved.

'The olive tree is surely the richest gift from heaven'
Thomas Jefferson

Oils

A 6,000-year history

There is evidence that olives were already being cultivated over 6,000 years ago. It is probable that the plant originated in Syria and it is thought to be very likely that the first people to transform the wild plant into a domestic crop spoke a Semetic language.

The journey of olive cultivation from Syria to the Aegean Islands and the sunny hills of Anatolia was relatively straightforward. From there, it travelled on to the rest of Greece where it enjoyed unexpected success and was put to uses that made it indispensible to the ancient peoples of the Mediterranean.

Olive trees were cultivated on the island of Crete from 2,500 BC, and the wealth of the Cretan king was certainly due in part to the export of olive oil to Egypt and the countries of the eastern coast of the Mediterranean. It also seems likely that the Greeks planted olive groves in the vast sunny and fertile area of Puglia, leading the Romans to name it Magna Graecia after the land fell into their hands. The Greeks are also thought to have planted olive groves in Calabria, Sicily and Campania.

Despite the widespread use of olive oil in classical times, there are still those who maintain that the first Italian region where olive trees were cultivated was Liguria, brought by the Crusades from Palestine after the year 1,000 AD. This theory is probably only true with regard to the particular type of olive tree that

In numerous passages from ancient poems such as The Iliad, The Odyssey *and* The Aeneid *there are references to athletes using olive oil for massage before competition, and to winners being awarded, among other prizes, an olive wreath. To this day in Greece, if you are victorious in examinations you are awarded a wreath of olive branches.*

prospers so well on the hard hillsides, unprotected from the west and east winds around the Gulf of Genoa.

The use of olive oil in cooking spread slowly westwards from the Eastern Mediterranean. The cultivation of olive trees specifically for this purpose travelled to Rome from Greece, via Southern Italy, after 580 BC when vines also arrived on the hills of Upper Lazio and Etruria.

ABOVE *A coloured engraving shows the holy olive tree at the Acropolis in Athens, Greece. Olives and olive oil have long been of great import in Greece and employed in a wide range of uses.*

FAR LEFT AND LEFT *These two mosaics depict the process of olive picking and pressing. As you can see, it is a labour-intensive process and remains so to this day. The mosaics hail from Saint-Romain-en-Gal, France. Though not counted among the world's biggest olive producers, olive oil still goes hand in hand with Provence and is frequently used in French cuisine.*

Olives and the Holy Land

Limestone-rich, dry and stony soil that is well exposed to the sun makes for perfect conditions in which to grow olives in abundance. This soil is to be found in the cities of Galilee, and tradition has it that the famous Mount of Olives faces Jerusalem.

The cultivation of olive groves brought great wealth to this corner of the world, since the tree is particularly hardy and grows up to 12 metres/40 feet tall. Each tree produces up to 120 kg/265 lbs. of olives, which would have yielded at least 25 litres/26 quarts of oil in those days. However, it took 10 years after planting before a good harvest and 30 years to reach its full potential.

Olives would be harvested in September or October, and the timings are still the same to this day. Long poles were used to shake the branches and any remaining olives were left for the poor. The olive is pinky purple in hue when it is ripe and it appears to shine. To this day, olive oil producers look for this quality in their olives.

In Palestine, the type of oil that we know today as extra virgin, was obtained without pressing the olives. Instead, olives were put into a large basket and the weight of the olives would cause them to release their precious oil. Some drawings show the olives placed in a dome-shaped space cut into the rock from which the oil trickled through a hole bored at the bottom. A further method was to pour hot water over the olives a number of times and to collect the oil that gathered on the surface of the water. This oil was considered first grade. The oil was then stored in earthenware jars in the cellars of rich and powerful people of the time. These jars filled with oil constituted the real riches of kings. Lists describing the quantity of oil kept at a palace belonging to the King of Israel in the ninth century BC were engraved in pottery and found during the excavation at Samaria in Palestine centuries later.

In Deuteronomy, the last of the five books of Moses, oil is considered to show prosperity, joy and friendship. It is also recognized as a symbol of strength and wisdom. Olive oil is still widely used in Middle Eastern cooking today, where it takes the place of butter and fat, as well as being used in personal hygiene and in the preparation of beauty products. The wood of the olive tree, with its beautiful colours, is strong and shiny, and has always been much sought after.

Olive oil was once used in the anointments of sovereigns and it is interesting to note that the word 'Christos', another name for Jesus, means 'anointed'.

The ancient empires of the Near East and the Mediterranean depended on the olive tree for their principal supply of oil. Indeed, the word 'oil' in all Western languages can be traced back through the Latin *oleum* and the Greek *elaion*, to the older Semitic word *ulu*. All of these words mean olive oil.

OPPOSITE ABOVE *A view of the Mount of Olives and the garden of Gethsemane in Jerusalem. Several olive trees in the garden have been found to be among the oldest known to science. DNA tests have proved that they all come from the same parent plant.*

OPPOSITE BELOW LEFT *These giant terracotta pots known as amphoras hail from Knossos, Crete, which is considered Europe's oldest city. The amphoras may have once been used to store olive oil. Stoppers are likely to have been used to protect the contents.*

OPPOSITE BELOW RIGHT *Absalom's Pillar on the lower slopes of the Mount of Olives in the Kidron Valley, Jerusalem.*

BELOW *This amphora, decorated in the black-figure style, depicts a trio of workers using long poles to shake the branches of the olive tree before gathering the fallen olives into baskets. It dates back to the sixth century BC and is currently on display at the British Museum, London.*

How olives grow

The true genetic origin of today's cultivated olive, *Olea europaea*, is not known. Some scientists believe that the 'European' olive, which is the only olea with sufficiently large fruit to be edible, is a hybrid between two or more distinct species.

Other scientists consider *Olea europaea* to represent just one group of widely diverse plants with ecotypes or subspecies that are located in different geographic areas across the globe.

In almost every location where cultivated olives grow, wild olive trees and shrubbery called oleaster also exist. These plants may be seedlings of cultivated varieties spread by birds and other wildlife feeding on the fruit, or they could be more mature forms of subspecies or ecotypes that already existed there before the introduction of the cultivated olive. All the olea genres have the same number of chromosomes, and crosses between many of them have been successful.

ABOVE LEFT *Most of the olive tree's stages of growth take place in spring, summer and autumn. Some of the buds will turn to blossom that then becomes fruit, while others will turn into shoots and then branches.*

CENTRE LEFT *An olive tree in bloom in late spring, Tuscany, Italy. Around one in 20 of the clusters of flowers will become an olive. The olives are picked six to eight months after the blossoms appear.*

CENTRE RIGHT *Certain types of olive like the French Picholine or the Spanish Manzanilla are best picked when they are green, since they are more flavoursome before reaching full maturity.*

ABOVE RIGHT *Other types of olives, such as the Niçoise or the Greek Kalamata, are best enjoyed when fully ripe. A purplish black colour and sheen are signs that the olives are ready to be picked.*

Now to talk about how the olive grows on the tree and its annual cycle. As we have discussed, there are hundreds of different varieties of olive. Like grapes, the variety grown depends on the climate, the soil and also whether the olives are to be pressed for oil or preserved for eating. With table olives, the firmness and fleshiness of the fruit is of the greatest importance, whereas olives grown for pressing must have a high oil content. All olives are green at first and turn pinky, purpley and then black when fully ripe; I find the changing colours of an olive rather wonderful to watch.

When I went olive picking (a lot of fun!), we were told to pick olives when they were marbled with pink and purple. Olives are fully ripe when they are purplish black in colour

and have that shiny quality. Certain types of olives, such as the Spanish Manzanilla and the French Picholine, are tastier when picked green. Others like the famous Niçoise and the Greek Kalamata are best when fully ripe. Climate is vital to the success of olive trees – the tree cannot tolerate extreme cold or damp, but can survive lengthy periods of drought. Therefore, the best conditions for olive trees to thrive is between the latitudes 25° and 45° N, and they flourish especially well in the Mediterranean climate with its mild winters and long, hot summers.

Trees can grow up to 15 metres/50 feet but are pruned back to about half that to facilitate the picking of the fruit. The tree's trunk, smooth and grey when young, becomes twisted and

ABOVE *A grove of olive trees in the garden of Gethsemane, Jerusalem, Israel. The trees are still able to bear fruit even at their advanced age, as shown by the gnarled trunks.*

RIGHT *As well as producing the wonderful olive fruit that is prized across the world, the leaves of the tree have their uses too. See pages 43 and 169 for ways to exploit their medicinal purposes.*

THESE PAGES *Olives flourish in dry, arid conditions such as those found here in Crete. The trees can survive long periods of drought but cannot tolerate extreme cold or damp weather, which is why olives are principally found in Mediterranean climes where the winters tend to be mild.*

gnarled over the years. It takes between five and eight years before an olive tree will bear its first fruit and then it can go on producing for many, many years to come. Olive trees have great tenacity because when the main trunk dies, new shoots appear at its base, eventually growing into a new tree. Carol Drinkwater has written about the oil trail and discovered that the trees in Syria are as old as 600 years and still bear fruit. Even the trees in the garden of Gethsemane remain strong and fruit bearing. New trees can be grown from seed but they take years to reach the

RIGHT *A botanical drawing of an olive plant,* Olea europea, *showing the arrangement and details of the leaves and flowers, as well as a cross-section of the fruit revealing the stone.*

fruit-bearing stage. The typical method of propagation is to take cuttings from mature trees. Some varieties have developed resistance to cold, others to pests and drought. Propagation from cuttings means the new tree will carry these resistances.

The olive is a stone fruit like the cherry or plum and it is the slender stone encased inside the fruit that contains the seed of the tree itself. Botanically, this type of fleshy fruit encasing a stone is known as a drupe. The tree is an evergreen and its leaves live for about three years before dying and making way for new ones. Olive leaves are paved opposite each other down the branches. They are single and undivided, rather like a willow leaf: lance-shaped, shiny and leathery. The upper surface is dark green and the lower surface appears to be silvery green, because it is covered with minute scales. This is why in the wind olive trees seem to shimmer in a silvery haze. The tree blooms in late spring with clusters of white flowers. Depending on the variety, there can be anything from ten to over 40 flowers in a cluster, but only one in every 20 flowers will become an olive. Even though olive trees are self-pollinating, it is very difficult for the flowers to achieve fertilization at the best of times, but the weather is the prime enemy. Rain at blossom time can be disastrous. As a result, fruit setting is erratic but it is improved by planting another variety of olive tree for cross-pollination.

Between June and October, fruition takes place. This is the time during which the stone (endocarp) hardens and the pulp (mesocarp) fills out. The flesh is encased by the skin (epicarp) and as the olive ripens the epicarp changes from green through

RIGHT *Harvest time in Puglia in Italy, which runs through November and December.*

BELOW *Olives being stripped from a branch with the aid of a small rake. They are usually 'combed' into nets laid on the ground below the trees to catch the falling olives.*

BOTTOM *The bounty of newly harvested olives. Green olives tend to produce a more bitter taste, while care must be taken to avoid overripe olives, which can taste rancid.*

OPPOSITE *In this traditional method of olive picking, olives are picked and dropped into the net. The lady on the left is separating the olives from any attached leaves and twigs.*

FAR LEFT *Olive production is often a family business. Here, a Palestinian boy shows off his pickings in Gaza. Olive picking remains a highly manual process to this day and is unlikely to ever be fully replaced by machinery.*

LEFT AND BELOW *Olive harvest season begins in Palestine at the beginning of October and lasts for a long period. However, the season is shorter than it once was and harvests will vary from year to year. Once picked, it is time to take the olives to a processing plant. It is best to extract the oil immediately after harvest for maximum flavour.*

violet and red to black. Six to eight months after the blossoms appear, the olives have maximum oil content; they are black and fully ripe.

Olive trees are mostly found in arid terrain; they need little rain and can survive in the poorest soil because the roots bore deep into the earth in search of what little moisture they require. In these conditions, they will produce a mediocre harvest. However, with care and attention the tree is far more productive and bears fruit every year rather than every other year.

Growing olives is now big business. Olive oil is a world commodity, so modern methods of cultivation are increasingly used, much like for other vital crops – and these days, on most commercial estates, trees are fertilized, pruned and irrigated.

In early autumn and spring, the soil in the groves is ploughed and weeded and the trees are pruned. Pruning is important but labour intensive; by thinning out the growth on the crown of the tree, the fruit-bearing branches can be exposed to the sun and air. The removal of vigorous but sterile branches and suckles, which appear in abundance at the base of the tree, means that the nutrients in the soil will be better utilized. A tree can yield 15–20 kg/30–44 lbs. of olives depending on how it is tended. Think of the work involved in going over every tree, laboriously and carefully one at a time, by hand. There can be no short cuts and there is no possible means of mechanized pruning. The olive grower's year is certainly a full and active one. Apart from pruning and fertilizing, they have to harvest and press the olives.

Like all fruit trees, the olive is subject to attack from fungi and insects. Its particular enemy is the olive moth, whose caterpillars will happily eat their way through leaves and buds. These enemies need to be controlled and so spraying with pesticides may be required. However, some producers choose to grow their olives organically because of concern over contamination of the fruit by pesticides.

The desired object of all this work is, of course, to produce a good crop of olives, but the bounty that the olive tree provides is not in its fruit alone. There is almost no part of this eternal tree that man cannot utilize. The prunings of the tree make excellent firewood – my grandfather said that the wood was a reward for tending the trees so well. The heat is second to none and ideal for a pizza oven. Olive wood is highly prized for its beautiful black and brown grain and its honey colour. I love all of my olive wood possessions – they are so special and beautiful to touch.

ABOVE *This large mill, found in Maussane-les-Alpilles, France, is pressing olives into oil for a local co-operative.*

RIGHT *A Palestinian worker places crushed olives between metal plates at a stone press in a village near Nablus in Palestine.*

Indeed, the Romans valued the wood so highly that they forbade its being burned for common use and reserved it solely for the altars of the gods. It is now fashioned into furniture, boxes, and more, and today, as in Greek times, it is used by craftsmen for making works of art.

As mentioned before, the tree's leaves are curative. Even the residue of stones and skin after pressing is used in many mills as feed and as fertilizer for the trees. Can there be another tree with such a history and folklore surrounding it?

Extracting olive oil

Illustrations on earthenware vases reveal that olives were first tested for ripeness and quality by squeezing the juice from a few olives through a funnel into a small bottle. The flavour and smell of the oil extracted in this way was then evaluated. Ancient vessels depicting this process are still on display in museums around the world.

Although it is best to extract the oil immediately after harvest, the olives were sometimes stored on the floor of the oil press. The first step was to separate the pulp from the stone and, given that olives have a fairly tough stone, the olives were crushed before they were pressed.

The method employed to crush the olives was very simple: the olives were placed in a container and a cylindrical stone was rolled backwards and forwards over them. The Roman olearia was a rolling mill made up of two cylindrical stones that were attached to the same horizontal axis, which was hinged, vertically, between them. When the central pivot was turned, the stones revolved rapidly at an adjustable distance above the flat container holding the olives. This method made it possible to separate the pulp without crushing the stones.

The oldest remains of an olive press were found in Crete and date back to 1,800–1,500 BC. A 'beam' press for olives was also found on one of the Cyclades Islands. This type of press is illustrated on many painted earthenware vases, particularly on the black-figure-style pottery made in 1,800–1,500 BC. The beam press worked on a lever system: one end of a beam was placed in an opening in a wall or between two stone pillars, while the other end was pulled downwards and often weighted with heavy stones. The olives, in sacks or between wooden planks, were crushed beneath the centre part of the beam.

The liquid obtained was left to settle in vats and the water let out through a tap/faucet at the bottom. The complete separation of the oil from the watery liquid is of utmost importance, since this liquid is bitter and could ruin the oil's flavour. The olives were then doused in hot water and pressed, the quality of the oil diminishing with each pressing.

Three qualities of oil would usually be produced: the first grade was for cooking; the other two for cosmetics or toiletries.

ABOVE *This is an olive crusher made from Vesuvian lava, in Pompeii, Italy. This contraption is designed to separate the pulp from the stone. Since the stone is fairly tough, the olives need to be crushed before being pressed.*

BELOW *Traditional terracotta pots used to store olives. Nowadays, olives are usually found packed in brine or oil to keep them fresh.*

OPPOSITE *The process from olive to oil comprises several stages. Olive oil tasting evenings are becoming increasingly popular and give you the opportunity to sample before buying. It is best not to smoke or brush your teeth before a tasting, as your palate will be affected. When tasting, swill the oil around your mouth before breathing in so as to fully appreciate the oil's fresh and fruity aromas.*

THIS PAGE *Although they are impressive at any hour of the day, there is something undeniably magical about venerable old olive trees at dusk.*

The New World

The 'New World', as it has come to be known, is experiencing a period of unprecedented growth in its olive oil markets, with Chile, Argentina, South Africa, Australia, New Zealand and the USA at the forefront. South Africa is worth singling out, as despite the youth of its market, it has picked up many international awards in recent years. Indeed, Morgenster Estate (see page 38) picked up the Best Blended Olive Oil in the world at the *L'extravirgine* competition held in Italy in 2005. At the New York International Olive Oil Competition in 2013, Italy and Spain topped the accolades, but it was the USA's third place haul of 36 awards that garnered much attention.

RIGHT *This young olive plantation in California is typical of those belonging to emerging New World producers who are making some ambitious and exciting oils.*

The huge investment in olive trees in the New World combined with the waiting time involved for high yields has led to detailed and rigorous processes, in turn resulting in a wide range of truly superb oils. This period of prolific growth in New World oils, most notably in Australia, Chile and the USA, has arrived at a time when some 'Old World' oil producers have become complacent and have allowed oil production standards to slip. Among the malpractices now being stamped out is that of piling olives high to rot for months before being processed, to facilitate greater extraction of the oil. And it is well documented that various seed oils, such as cotton, hemp, sesame, palm nut, sunflower and hazelnut, have been used to adulterate olive oil to make it cheaper. Indeed, the development of the International Olive Oil Council was in part due to the presence of widespread fraud in the olive oil trade, and specifically, the fradulent sale of olive pomace oil, marketed as extra virgin olive oil.

The provisional figure for total world production of olive oil in 2013–14 was 3,098,000 tonnes. The EU accounts for a colossal 2,038,000 tonnes out of the total figure, comprising the three biggest producing countries in the world. In first place, by a staggering distance is Spain with 1,536,600 tonnes – just a fraction under half of total world production. Italy takes the silver medal with 450,000 tonnes, followed by Greece, with 230,000 tonnes. Outside the EU, the largest producers are Turkey (180,000 tonnes), Syria (135,000 tonnes), Morocco (120,000 tonnes), Tunisia (80,000 tonnes) and Algeria (62,000 tonnes).

Out of the 2013–14 provisional world production total, the Old World accounts for 3,005,000 tonnes and the New World 93,000 tonnes. This doesn't tell the whole story, though, as while Old World production has hovered around the 3,000,000 tonne mark for the last 10 years, back in 2003, New World production was only a quarter what it was today. The last 10 years has seen an unprecedented growth in existing New World olive oil producers as well as the welcome emergence of new producers. A good case in point is Australia, which only begun producing olive oil in 1998 (500 tonnes was recorded for that year). By contrast, its provisional figure for 2013–14 is 18,000 tonnes. Likewise, Chile only entered the market in 2006–7, and recorded a provisional figure of 32,000 tonnes for 2013–14. A similar picture can be painted of the USA, now producing a remarkable ten times what it was ten years' ago. It is an encouraging scene, as the upward trend is sure to continue, with more and more new plantations yielding for the first time in the coming years.

Types of oil

As you will no doubt have noticed from visiting your local supermarket, a vast variety of different oils are available to buy these days. I highly recommend having a range to choose from in your store cupboard as they serve myriad purposes – from salad dressings and marinades to a base for homemade mayonnaise.

Almond oil

This is a pale, clean oil with a fairly neutral flavour and, rather surprisingly, not much of an almond taste. It is mainly used in baking and confectionery. I find it useful for oiling baking pans or soufflé dishes when making very delicately flavoured sponges or soufflés, or for oiling a marble slab on the rare occasions when I make sweets/candy. Used alone, it is not enough to give an almond flavour to cakes and biscuits/cookies. For that you need to use almond essence, or, of course, almonds themselves.

Avocado oil

Extracted from the inedible stone of the avocado, this is a very neutral oil. It is almost colourless and aromaless. It has no flavour of the rich buttery avocado, although it does feel and taste like a very oily oil.

Corn oil

This is one of the most economical and widely used of all edible oils. It is a deepish, golden yellow with quite a strong flavour. It is technically suitable for all culinary uses including baking, but is not pleasant in salad dressings and mayonnaise. For frying I prefer an oil that is lighter in texture, such as groundnut/peanut or sunflower oil.

Fruit oils

These differ from the other oils in that they are used for flavour and not for emulsifying (as in mayonnaise), lubricating (as in salad dressings) or cooking (as in deep-frying). They are the essential oils stored in the skin of citrus fruits. Grapefruit, lemon and sweet orange oil are remarkable for their aroma and concentration. Just a drop is needed to permeate a dish with the scent and flavour of the fruit. I use them with a dash of spirit such as gin or vodka to flavour a sauce for fish or chicken. They are delicious stirred into custards or creams for cake filling. They are less successful when cooked in cake batters, for example, since they are so volatile that they simply disappear.

Grapeseed oil

A pale, delicate, quite neutral but pleasant-tasting oil, extracted from grape pips, that is quite widely available. It is excellent for frying and for general culinary use, and it is my favourite oil for making mayonnaise. If you want to use hazelnut or sesame oil but find them too strong, then grapeseed oil is excellent for diluting them to your preferred concentration.

Groundnut/Peanut oil

This is a very fine oil for all culinary uses – frying, baking, salad dressings and mayonnaise. It is used a great deal in French and Chinese kitchens, which is certainly an indication of its quality.

Hazelnut oil

An expensive but delicious oil, this is one of the many nut oils that are now becoming more readily available. It is too expensive to use on anything but the finest salads, with very little well-aged wine vinegar or lemon juice added, and maybe a few crushed hazelnuts. It is a richly flavoured, nutty brown oil that marries beautifully with fish, for example as a marinade for a raw fish salad that is then served with the marinade. I have also, extravagantly, used it as the shortening when baking with ground hazelnuts. It works very well, but some of the flavour is lost when the oil is heated. However, it has such a powerful flavour to begin with that there is always more than enough left.

Rapeseed/Canola oil

Bright yellow fields of rapeseed produce Britain's only home-grown source of edible oil. It was introduced as a crop by the Romans to provide oil, since olives would not grow in Britain.

It is a bland, neutrally flavoured oil, suitable for frying, baking and other uses. It is lower in saturated fats than most other commonly used fats. It is sometimes inaccurately called mustard oil because the rape plant, like mustard, is a member of the brassica family and confusingly has very similar yellow flowers.

Sesame seed oil

Cold-pressed, unblended sesame oil has a rich, light brown colour, a distinctive smell and a strong, nutty flavour. Indeed, many people find it too strong and so a teaspoon mixed with a couple of tablespoons of grapeseed oil is sufficient. Sesame oil keeps extremely well, since it contains a substance that prevents it from going rancid.

Toasted sesame oil, which has a deep golden colour, is an important ingredient in Japanese and Chinese cooking. It is used more as a seasoning, flavouring or marinating ingredient than as a cooking medium, as the oil burns at a relatively low temperature.

Sunflower oil

Sunflower oil is perhaps the best all-purpose oil. It is tasteless and pale yellow, also light in texture, which makes it excellent for frying, as an ingredient in salad dressings and as the oil for mayonnaise, mixed with other more highly flavoured oils if desired.

Walnut oil

This deliciously nutty oil is made in France – in the Dordogne, Perigord and the Loire – and also in Italy. Production is small-scale, and it is therefore an expensive oil. It does not keep too well and once opened it should be stored in a cool place to prevent it from turning rancid, but not in the refrigerator, as this can cause it to solidify and change colour.

It is wonderful on salads, mixed with only a hint of good vinegar or lemon juice and a few crushed walnuts. It adds extra depth of flavour in baking. Try it in a walnut and coffee cake, in breakfast breads with a chopped walnut and raisin mixture, in pastry for a walnut tart, or to make walnut biscuits. Mix with lime juice and onions for a marvellous marinade for raw fish. You can also use it to flavour chicken sauces and marinades, and it is delicious with warm vegetables.

Cooking with oil

Although many people fry with extra virgin olive oil, I would never recommend it, as the heat causes the oil to burn and release free radicals. I find also that the flavour of the oil from frying is destroyed, along with the nutrition and goodness. However, I'm sure that some people will dispute this!

chilli oil

sunflower oil

hazelnut oil

sesame oil

I will always use a basic olive oil or groundnut oil for frying. Groundnut oil is great at withstanding high temperatures, and is a good option for obtaining colour on food and heating up quickly. It is used a great deal in Asian cooking. As with all other fats and oils, it must never be allowed to smoke when heated. This is a sign of overheating – the oil turns black and forms acrolein, which is toxic.

You may sometimes see olive oil with a white solid layer at the bottom of the bottle. This happens when it has been exposed to the cold and will not damage or change the oil in any way. If a solid layer does form, simply return the oil to room temperature and it will return to normal. Nevertheless, it's best not to store oils in the refrigerator.

rapeseed/canola oil

walnut oil

groundnut oil

coconut oil

An introduction to oil tasting

Olive oil tastings are becoming popular events, run by cookery schools, wine stores or delicatessens. They allow sampling before buying and give you the opportunity to compare different oils. They are such fun and are an excellent way for you to discover your personal preferences before investing in a bottle. Just a couple of tips: I often eat an apple or a little fennel to cleanse my palate before tasting oil; also please try not to smoke or brush your teeth before a tasting, as it will ruin your palate. The enjoyment of great oil, I believe, is in swilling the oil around your mouth, before closing your mouth and breathing in to appreciate it. You will then truly be able to enjoy the oil with all of its fresh and fruity aromas.

According to Anne Dolamore, author of *The Essential Olive Oil Companion*, it is often difficult to find the words to describe different flavours of oil, so the International Olive Oil Council has drawn up a general basic vocabulary for use by professional tasters, as a way of establishing standards of the organoleptic assessment of virgin olive oils.

Grades of olive oil as designated by the International Olive Oil Council

Extra virgin olive oil
This is virgin olive oil of absolutely perfect taste and odour, having maximum acidity in terms of oleic acid of 1 g per 100 g or, more simply, with an acidity of less than 1 per cent.

Virgin oil
This is virgin oil of absolutely perfect taste and odour, but possessing a maximum acidity in terms of oleic acid of 1.5 g per 100 g or acidity of less than 1.5 per cent.

Virgin olive oil lampante (lamp oil)
This is an off-taste and off-smelling virgin olive oil with an acidity in terms of oleic of more than 3.3 g per 100 g, i.e. 3 per cent. It is intended for refining or for technical purposes.

Olive oil
This is the oil I use mainly to cook with. This is olive oil obtained from virgin olive oils by refining methods.

Olive residue oil
This is a crude oil obtained by treating olive residues with solvents and is intended for subsequent refining prior to human consumption.

Main constituents of olive oil
Monounsaturated fatty acids (oleic) 56–83%
Saturated fatty acids 8–23.5%
Polyunsaturated unfatty acids (linoleic) 3.5–20%
Stearic acids 0.5–5%
Polyunsaturated fatty acids (linolenic) 0–1.5%
Note: olive oil also contains small quantities of vitamin E and Provitamin A (carotene)

Oil vocabulary as drawn up by the International Olive Oil Council

- Almond – this flavour is divided in two: fresh almond and rancid bitter almond
- Apple
- Bitter
- Bitter green leaves
- Brine
- Burned
- Cucumber
- Earthy/muddy
- Flat
- Fruity
- Grass
- Harsh
- Hay
- Metallic
- Musty
- Old
- Rancid
- Rough
- Sweet
- Winey-Vinegary

I urge you to develop your own flavour and tasting glossary, as we are all so different and we may in fact detect different notes.

There are so many varieties of olives that I have named only a few here that are quite common:

- Manzanilla
- Nicoise
- Kalamata
- Arbequina
- Gordal

- Mission
- Lugano
- Hojiblanca
- Royal
- Picholine

- Cerasuola
- Nocellara
- Biancolilla

Table olives

In our pursuit to find the best olive oil, we must not forget that the fruit itself offers many tastes when preserved whole. There are delectable ranges of table olives – green and black; smooth and hard; large and fleshy; stoned/pitted or stuffed with pimento, almonds, anchovy, capers or garlic; packed in brine or loose in oil and aromatic or cracked in the Greek style – the variety is enormous.

Just to journey through the Mediterranean sampling locally prepared olives would offer the traveller an exquisite multi-sensory experience. When the olives first start to form on the tree, they contain no oil, only a mixture of organic acids and sugars. By the magic of nature, a transformation gradually occurs as the olive ripens. A chemical process, called lipogenesis, slowly turns the acids and sugars into oil as the olive turns from palest green through rose to violet and black. Olives can be picked at any stage through the process, and the degree of ripeness will determine its taste.

You will have noticed the difference in taste between a green and black olive. You may like one but not the other. Green olives have very little oil; their flesh is firm because they aren't yet ripe, and they have a sharp tang. Black olives are full of oil, the flesh is soft because they are ripe and they have a mellower flavour. Green olives, because they are unripe, are inedible unless treated to remove the bitter glucosides. This is done on a commercial basis by immersing the olives in a soda solution and then washing them thoroughly in clean water, after which they are packed in brine. During this process the olives must be kept away from the air, to prevent them turning brown through oxidation. For centuries, however, the growers who prepare their own olives have simply washed them every day for about 10 days in fresh water and then immersed them in brine, which is often mixed with herbs, lemon or other aromatic ingredients. These combinations of herbs and aromatics can vary from region to region, even from family to family, and there are many secret recipes that have been passed down from generation to generation.

Black olives in contrast only need washing and preserving in brine or dry salt, as they are fully ripe.

Most consumers will not be in a position to treat fresh olives from their own trees, but you can buy stoned/pitted or whole green and black olives, loose or packed in brine, and preserve them in a variety of ways yourself. If you should, however, manage to obtain fresh olives, then you simply immerse them in cold water and change the water every 10 days. Then make a brine solution using about 500 g/1 lb. 2 oz. of salt to 5 kg/11 lbs. of olives. You can check that the strength of the solution is correct by seeing if an egg will float in it. Leave the olives in this solution for 3–4 weeks. They are then ready to enjoy.

Italian extra virgin olive oil

Colonna: Molise, Italy

The Colonna's Bosco Pontoni Estate is in the Molise, that little known region opposite Rome on the Adriatic Coast. Here, Prince Francesco, Marina Colonna's father, whose ancestors included notorious warriors and Pope Martin V, planted many different varieties of olive, some local varieties and some brought in from other regions. When her father died, Marina took over oil production. She has inherited his passion for growing good olives, and in this quest enlisted the help of the famous agronomist from Perugia University, Professor Fontanazza. Her oil has won many prizes over the years.

The estate oil has a beautifully aromatic nose, with strong green notes of sorrel and fresh-cut grass, which mingle in the mouth with flavours of woody herb stalks. The oil has a pleasant creaminess, balanced by hazelnut-skin bitterness, and a strong peppery warmth on the finish.

The organic oil has slightly more intensity than the estate, with a lovely undertone of warm dark/bittersweet chocolate and scents of unripe banana skin and raw artichoke. The flavour develops to a complex orange-pith bitterness with some woody herb elements and a long and intense cayenne pepper finish.

The Molise DOP oil, made with certified varieties typical to the region – Leccino and Gentile di Larino – has a wonderful aroma of sun-warmed rosemary that leaps out of the bottle, followed by ripe nectarines and warm hay. Sweet herbaceous flavours are nicely balanced by a woody bitterness and an aftertaste of more sweet herbs and salad leaves, leading to a red chilli/chile finish.

Badia a Coltibuono: Tuscany, Italy

The house oil, Cultus Boni, is a blend of oil produced on the estate, along with some that comes from neighbouring farms. It is typically Tuscan in style, with aromas of rocket/arugula, sorrel and a touch of mint, all balanced by a fine peppery finish.

The Campo Corto grove, planted at an altitude of 450 metres/1,300 feet in the pristine environment of the Badia forests, has been under organic cultivation since 1999. It is planted with the traditional Tuscan Frantoio variety. The olives are pressed on the day they are picked and make an oil that is emerald green in colour and with an intense aroma. The taste is grassy, with hints of artichoke and aromatic herbs, and the bitter almond and peppery finish is classically Tuscan. It is unfiltered and organic.

The Albareto groves are also part of the estate, and are planted with Frantoio, Moraiolo, Leccino and Pendolino varieties. These produce an oil with an intense herbaceous aroma with hints of asparagus and herbs, a verdant taste and peppery finish. Production is very limited. For example, in 2010 each tree yielded less than half a litre/quart of oil, and even in a good year the producers do not expect much more than 1 litre/quart from each of their 7,000 trees.

Frescobaldi: Tuscany, Italy

Florentine bankers since medieval times, the Frescobaldis were also treasurers to the English court at the end of the 13th century, and lent vast sums to Edward I and Edward II. After differences with the monarch forced them out of England, however, the Frescobaldis took their revenge, blockading the court's wine supply by commandeering the King's French wine shipments, leaving the court dry until the following year's harvest. Records do not show if they supplied the royal court with olive oil, but they were certainly producers at the time.

After the severe frosts in Tuscany in 1985, a group of producers set up a marketing group up under the Laudemio banner, as a guarantee of provenance and quality. The Frescobaldis were one of the instigators of Laudemio, and the oils were launched first in Florence and then in the UK at two events, one at the River Café, and one at the Italian embassy.

The Frescobaldis have their mill at Camperiti, down the road from their beautiful Castello di Nipozzano, and it is here that they press the olives, Frantoio (70 per cent), Moraiolo (20 per cent) and Leccino (10 per cent). The olives are harvested by hand and pressed in the family mill, after which some of the oil is stored in terracotta-glazed vases and the rest in stainless steel tanks (which have largely taken over from the traditional terracotta). The oil is then boxed to keep it out of the light.

The consistently outstanding Frescobaldi Laudemio has excellent balance, with a delicious aroma of fresh-cut grass, unripe banana and some darker notes of bitter chocolate. It is a superbly smooth oil, with flavours of bitter leaves and green apple peel growing into a warm, peppery spice, and a long finish.

Ravida: Sicily, Italy

The unmistakable Ravida smell leaps out of the bottle, intense with fresh herby hay, green tomatoes and sorrel. This carries through into the mouth, with more green tomatoes and grass, and some crushed woody herbs. The pepper grows to a sudden strong burst, yet does not overwhelm.

The estate's organic oil has more pungency and fresh bitterness, with strong notes of sorrel and raw artichoke, mingled with some eucalyptus notes. A very powerful oil, which has an intensely peppery finish that continues in the mouth long after swallowing.

This 'everyday' oil was blended by Natalia Ravida to give her consumers a versatile and inexpensive oil for cooking and making assertively flavoured dressings. It is aromatic and fruity with some gentle bitterness and peppery rocket/arugula on the finish, softened by notes of ripe tomato.

The family farm of La Gurra used to be vast, covering acres of land to the west of the small town of Menfi, in southwest Sicily. Over the years, some land has been divided up and sold off, but there is still a considerable area of cultivated olive trees, of vines and of lemon trees, as well as wild open spaces of the beautiful Sicilian macchia, full of aromatic herbs and ancient wild olive trees.

The modern mill is here at La Gurra, put in by Natalia's father, and so is the old stone one. No longer used, it is a memorial to her grandfather, who spent much of his time in the old farmhouse there, rather than in the beautiful grand villa in the centre of Menfi where Natalia's parents live.

Viola: Umbria, Italy

This certified organic oil is made primarily from Moraiolo olives with some Frantoio and Lecchino olives added to the mix. It is strongly herbaceous on the nose, with strong notes of fresh-cut grass and raw artichoke. Flavours of watercress offer a pleasant bitterness, balanced by a kick of chilli/chile at the finish. This is a powerful oil to enliven dishes such as a bean soup or avocado salad.

The business of making olive oil has been passed down through four generations of the Viola family, after they established their own mill in 1917. Located in the rocky terrain of the Assisi-Spoleto hills, in the beautiful region of Umbria, Italy, the Viola farm is now in the very capable hands of Marco Viola. Here, they produce not only their wonderful olive oil, but also a whole range of legumes and cereals. The family are strongly guided by organic farming principles, and strive to keep traditional farming methods alive, which they complement with up-to-date machinery where necessary. Every year the same team of pickers, many of whom are now elderly, descend on the farm to harvest the olive crop by hand to avoid bruising.

Marco produces four oils from his 21,000 trees. They are consistently outstanding, and we regularly receive emails detailing the latest award the family has won. Perhaps the greatest to date comes from *Flos Olei* – the most respected annual guide to olive oil – which awarded Viola the prestigious accolade of 'Mill of the Year 2012'.

Racalia: Sicily, Italy

Racalia is the estate surrounding Villa Ingham, which has been owned by the same English family since 1840. The estate stands on a west-facing ridge between Marsala and Trapani in Western Sicily. The formal gardens look out over the Mediterranean to the Stagnone and Egadi Islands. The olive groves, together with the orange and lemon groves, have become a significant producer of both high-quality olive oil and citrus fruits.

The olive groves are owned and managed directly by the family. Each and every olive is grown on the Racalia estate. No other olives are included in the make-up of Racalia olive oil. At harvest time, every evening the tons of olives picked during the day are taken to the olive press operated by award-winning organic olive oil producers, the Titone family.

Racalia olive oil is graded by a number of other properties and characteristics now laid down by the European Union. The finest olives are used to produce extra virgin olive oil in a carefully measured blend from native Sicilian Cerasuola, Nocellara and Biancolilla olive trees. One of the important elements is whether an oil is 'cold pressed'. To qualify as 'cold pressed', oil must be extracted at no more than 28°C(82°F). Racalia olive oil is pressed at a temperature lower than that, the result of which is a smaller quantity of a much finer olive oil.

French extra virgin olive oil

Alziari: Nice, France

This mild and delicate oil is made from the native small, maroon-coloured Cailletier olive. In the interests of full disclosure, however, we do believe that the producers buy in some oil to add to the mix. Ideal for use in cooking or making mayonnaise, it has a rich, buttery texture, with gentle flavours of ripe avocado and banana, and some creamy almond notes on the finish. Even if it is not made entirely from Niçoise olives, it is Niçoise in style.

Jacques Médecin, late mayor of Nice, was commented on by Rowley Leigh, chef and food writer for the *Financial Times*:

'Things changed in 1983 with the publication of the English translation of *Cuisine Niçoise: Recipes from a Mediterranean Kitchen* by one Jacques Médecin. In spite of the fact that Médecin was a famously racist mayor of Nice who was extradited from South America in order to face trial on corruption charges, the book, unlike its author, was a delight... However crooked Médecin had been, none of us doubted his cooking'. What's the connection between Médecin and Alziari? A tin of Alziari oil is illustrated on the front cover of Médecin's aforementioned book.

Greek extra virgin olive oil

Odysea Iliada: Kalamata, Greece

This oil is produced in the Kalamata region of the Peloponnese, southern Greece, from the Koroneiki olive. Grassy green in colour, with a full and complex flavour, this excellent-value oil is useful both for cooking and for salad dressings where you might use balsamic vinegar and mustard as an emulsifier. Notes of tropical fruits such as passion fruit and mango mingle with some herbaceous notes that keep the oil fresh, with a nice peppery finish. It was given POD status in 1997, which guarantees that the olives are grown and pressed in the Kalamata region.

Odysea started as a single stall on the Portobello Road Market in West London, selling nothing but Greek olives. As the stall gained popularity, its proprietor, Panos Manuelides, saw that there was a growing market in the UK for high-quality Greek produce. From there, the company has gone from strength to strength, and now imports a dazzling array of Greek products. These are good-quality, good value olive oils that bridge an often difficult gap between everyday cooking oil and some of the more unique, single estate-bottled oils.

Spanish extra virgin olive oil

Marqués de Valdueza: Extremadura, Spain

The first oil of the Valdueza Estate in Extremadura, western Spain, is a blend of Arbequina, Picual, Hojiblanca and Marisca olives. It has a pretty aroma, with top notes of mango and papaya and some deeper tones of tomato leaves. It has a lovely creamy texture in the mouth with sweet cobnut flavours balanced by a nice walnut-skin bitterness. This is a versatile oil, perfect for dressing fish or fresh vegetables.

The Merula, housed in a superbly designed, award-winning tin, is the estate's second oil. Tangerine, apple peel and ripe tomatoes give way to a nutty creaminess in the mouth, balanced with more ripe tomatoes and fresh Cos/Romaine lettuce. The estate completes its range with the Almazara Perales, a superb cooking oil, with enough flavour to use in light dressings too.

Can Martina: Ibiza

At this small olive grove, the olives are hand picked and pressed within two hours. This gives the oil the strong flavour loved by connoisseurs, with lots of antioxidants, low acidity and no cholesterol. At present only about 2,000 litres/2,100 quarts of oil are produced per vintage, but this will gradually increase as the trees get larger and more productive.

New World extra virgin olive oils

Morgenster: Somerset West, South Africa

Set in the Western Cape region of South Africa, the Morgenster estate nestles in the foothills of the Helderberg mountains, where former cloth merchant Giulio Bertrand has planted Italian olive varieties to make this internationally acclaimed oil, along with his vineyards and an olive tree nursery. The oil has consistently gained 97 points in the respected *Flos Olei Olive Oil Guide* since 2010, and is rightly regarded as one of the best in the world. Ever at the forefront of technological advances, Bertrand has built a long-term partnership with the Olive Oil Research Institute of Italy, from which he imports the world's most up-to-date olive tree cultivars and production technology.

The nose is fresh and grassy, with notes of walnut skins and ripening tomatoes. Salad leaves mingle with a softer nutty note in the mouth, balanced by a peppery rocket/arugula hitting the back of the throat and uplifting bitter leaf flavours.

The Village Press: Hawke's Bay, New Zealand

The olive groves are located among Hawke's Bay's vineyards, fruit-filled orchards and rich agricultural land, near The Village Press olive pressing facility. The 30,000 olive trees, grown over 45 hectares/110 acres are thriving in Hawke's Bay's sunshine, adequate rainfall and free-draining soil profiles – making for ideal olive growing conditions. Coming from the fruit of a single variety of olive tree (Barnea, Manzanillo, Picual, Frantoio, Leccino), the oil is unfiltered, so it retains its full flavour and nutritional qualities, and is additive-free.

Their Frantoio olive oil is complex, balanced, and intense, with fresh herb, green olive and sweet fruit aromas. It makes outstanding basil or coriander/cilantro pesto, lifting the distinctive herb flavours to a different level. The oil is thick and chocolatey, making it an ideal accompaniment for a sourdough bread or fresh focaccia.

Their Manzanillo olive oil is a big, bright Chardonnay of olive oils. It is cold-pressed, with fresh and herbaceous flavours that are very well balanced, light-bodied and spicy. This New World oil is a firm favourite in my kitchen.

ENZO Olive Oil Company: California, USA

The Ricchiuti family have been working the land of California for 100 years. Vincenzo Ricchiuti planted the first family acreage in 1914 with grapes and figs. Over the years they built up a reputation for growing delicious citrus fruits, peaches, plums, apricots, nectarines, grapes and almonds, but it was only in 2008 that Vicenzo's grandson Patrick and his great-grandson Vincent entered the olive oil business. In 2011, they harvested their first crop of organic olives and created ENZO Organic Extra Virgin Olive Oil. The 'Delicate' (they also have 'Medium' and 'Bold') 100% estate-grown olive oil has subtle zesty notes of dry grass and browned toast, leading into a mild peppery finish.

According to *The New York Times*, 10 years ago the California olive oil trade, which had efffectively been started by 16th-century Spanish missionaries, was almost dead, except for a handful of small-scale producers. However, times have changed and the success of this young brand is a really promising sign for the future of Californian olive oil production.

Olio Santo: California, USA

Produced at the Talcott Ranch in Carneros, Napa Valley for the last 18 years, Olio Santo is one of California's oldest olive oils. In ancient times, olio santo (Italian for 'sacred oil') was made from the best olives of the olive harvest and was reserved for use in religious ceremonies. With a name like Olio Santo, this extra virgin olive oil has a lot to live up to, and it does not disappoint. It is a full-bodied oil, with a robust early-harvest flavour and has won many fans including Ina Garten, the American author and Emmy Award-winning host of the Food Network programme *Barefoot Contessa*. She even lists Olio Santo as one of the seven staple ingredients to be included in every home chef's pantry. It's suitable for all uses, from salad dressings to sautés, and won't overpower delicate flavours.

Pressed from a selection of Tuscan varietals that thrive in the hot days and cooler nights of the Carneros region, Olio Santo has been the top-selling olive oil at US gourmet store Williams-Sonoma for nearly two decades. It is an award-winning combination of old-world varietals in a breathtaking New World location.

Infused extra virgin olive oils

Lunaio basil-infused extra virgin olive oil, Tuscany, Italy
This is an organic stone-milled basil oil, delicate and balanced with a glorious colour. Surprisingly light in flavour so as not to be overpowering, it lends itself to being extremely versatile in the kitchen. Produced in Tuscany by a well-respected producer, this oil is a must for salads and a perfect partner for bread.

Il Boschetto rosemary-infused extra virgin olive oil, Maremma, Tuscany
Produced in the Maremma region of Tuscany, this oil is magnificently scented with rosemary. Only 1% rosemary is needed, which just goes to show how the sunshine intensifies the flavour. A natural partner with lamb, this oil is well balanced, using excellent-quality oil as its backbone. Serve it alongside good breads to show its wonderful flavour off.

DOS Tartufi: Umbria, Italy
Emanuele Musini has developed a method of getting the natural aroma of the truffle or the porcini mushroom into the oil without either steeping the fungi in the oil, which can create a risk of botulism, or by using a chemical essence that mimics the aroma but is not actually the aroma. He is coy about how he actually does it, but he has done it well. No more of those slightly petrolly aromas that used to be associated with truffle oil. Use over mushroom risottos, cold chicken, dripped into fresh mayonnaise, in mashed potatoes – the list is endless.

Nudo extra virgin olive oil with Sicilian chillies, Marche, Italy
Southern chillies/chiles are certainly more distinctive in flavour, and this oil is particularly good. The oil comes from a small farm in the Marche region, in northeast Italy, and the chillies/chiles are sourced for their heat and flavour. The infusion takes three weeks, which leads to a gentle kick upon tasting. This is a worthy oil to use with all pasta, pizza, red meats and egg dishes. The production is small, lending itself to a well-produced and balanced oil.

Making your own herb oils

Herb oils are extremely simple to make and they look and smell as delicious as they taste. Experiment with different herbs, using the leaf part only. Particularly lovely herb oils can be made using basil, rosemary, tarragon, thyme and of course, for beauty preparations, lavender. If possible, make your herb oils in summer, as strong sunlight is needed for the aromatic oils of the herbs to mingle with the oil itself.

Crush the herbs using a pestle and mortar. Alternatively, put them through a blender or food processor. Then put 2 tablespoons of the crushed herbs into a 300-ml/10-fl. oz. bottle. Add olive oil, filling the bottle only three-quarters full. Add 1 tablespoon of wine vinegar and cork the bottle tightly.

Put the bottle somewhere where it receives hot sunlight and leave it there for two or three weeks, shaking the bottle a couple of times a day. At the end of this time, strain off the oil and press any remaining oil out of the crushed herbs. Repeat the process – using freshly cut herbs – until the oil is strong enough. You should be able to really smell the herb when you put a little of the oil onto the back of your hand.

If there is not enough sun to bring the flavour out of the herbs, then you can put the bottles – tightly corked of course – into a double boiler and 'cook' them at just below boiling point for a few hours each day. The oil should be strong enough after seven or eight days of this treatment.

Finally, add a sprig of the dried herb for decoration.

Olive oil and health

For centuries, the nutritional, cosmetic and medicinal benefits of olive oil have been recognized by the people of the Mediterranean. In the Bible, for instance, its healing powers are amply demonstrated in the famous parable where the Good Samaritan tends to the robbed man by pouring oil and wine into his wounds.

In Greek and Roman times, people cleaned their skin by rubbing themselves with olive oil, then scraping it off with a curved blade of wood or bronze called a strigil. In the British Museum today, there is a fine example of a bronze pot for holding olive oil with two strigils, as used by Greek athletes. Olive oil was also used to maintain the suppleness of skin and muscle, to heal abrasions and to soothe the burning and drying effects of sun and wind. Women used it especially to give body and shine to their hair. Mixed with spices or herbs, it was administered both internally and externally for health and beauty.

Both Pliny and Hippocrates prescribed medications containing olive oil and olive leaves as cures for a number of disorders ranging from inflammation of the gums, insomnia and nausea to boils. Many of these old remedies have passed into folk medicine and are still as relevant today as they were hundreds of years ago.

Recent research has now provided firm proof that a Mediterranean-style diet, which includes olive oil, is not only generally healthy, but that consuming olive oil can actually reduce cholesterol levels.

The increase in heart disease since the war was an alarming indicator that something in the contemporary industrialized lifestyle was to blame. This led the American Heart Foundation to initiate research into the modern diet, smoking, obesity and high blood pressure. They found that in Greece, and especially on the island of Crete, the mortality rate due to cardiovascular illnesses was the lowest in the world – while Finland and the United States had the highest coronary mortalities. The only variable in the populations studied proved to be the type of fat ingested. In the countries with the highest incidences of cardiovascular diseases, saturated fats were consumed most often and these fats were discovered to cause an increase in cholesterol levels. Monounsaturates, on the other hand, contain no cholesterol. Over the last 20 years, a number of medical congresses, promoted by the International Olive Oil Council, have studied the role of fats in the human diet. These have revealed what an important role olive oil has to play in maintaining good health.

Fats or lipids are essential in a well-balanced diet. They can be divided into saturates and unsaturates, depending on whether they have simple or double bonds between their carbon groups. Fatty acids with one double bond are called monounsaturates, whereas those with multiple double bonds are known as polyunsaturates. Olive oil and other vegetable oils contain unsaturated fatty acids, like oleic acid and linoleic acid. Olive oil actually comprises 80% oleic acid, placing it at the top of the list of monounsaturated fats. The two main polyunsaturated fatty acids are linoleic and linolenic acid, and these are found in large quantities in sunflower and corn oils. Saturated fatty acids, on the other hand, are found in animal fats, such as butter and lard.

Low-fat diets have long been recommended to reduce cholesterol. This meant cutting down on the intake of animal fats and using polyunsaturated fats in the form of vegetable oil.

Polyunsaturated fats have been heavily promoted over the last few years as the answer to a balanced fat intake, but in 1986 the results of research into monounsaturated fatty acids revealed some startling new evidence about the nature of cholesterol. There are two types, low density and high density. Low-density lipoproteins (LDL) transport and deposit cholesterol in the tissues and arteries. LDL increases with a high intake of saturated fatty acids and is therefore harmful because it will deposit more cholesterol. High-density lipoproteins (HDL) eliminate cholesterol from the cells, and carry it to the liver, where it is passed out through the bile ducts. While polyunsaturates reduce both LDL and HDL, monounsaturates reduce LDL while increasing HDL. An increase in the level of HDL will not only provide protection against cholesterol deposits, but it will also actually reduce cholesterol levels in the body.

All this evidence has been supported by numbers of studies conducted in Spain and the USA. Volunteers were put on diets using only olive oil, and then compared to another group who used only sunflower oil. The research showed that those using olive oil significantly increased their levels of HDL. Olive oil as the main source of monounsaturated fatty acids has to be the best form of fat to use.

The healthy aspects of olive oil are not only limited to its efficacy with regard to the heart. Research has also taken place over the years into its many other positive benefits on the human body. The oil, taken heated or unheated, has been shown to reduce gastric acidity, and its emollient effect protects against ulcers and aids the passage of food through the intestines. In other words, it helps prevent constipation. It also stimulates bile secretion and provokes contraction of the gallbladder, reducing the risk of gallstones.

Since olive oil contains vitamin E and oleic acid, which is also found in human milk, it aids normal bone growth and is most suitable for both expectant and nursing mothers because it encourages development of the infant's brain and nervous system before and after birth.

Finally, as if this combination of attributes was not enough, olive oil has also been shown to prevent the wear and tear of age on the functioning of the brain and on the ageing of the tissues and organs in general.

All this mountain of evidence proves conclusively that olive oil, of all the fats available, is highly beneficial to you whatever your age or lifestyle.

Folk remedies

For shiny hair After shampooing, rub a mixture of olive oil, egg yolk, juice of a lemon and a little beer into your hair. Leave for 5 minutes before washing it out.

To prevent dandruff Rub a mixture of olive oil and Eau de Cologne into the hair, then rinse.

For dry skin Make a face mask with an avocado and olive oil. Leave for 10 minutes and then rinse off.

To prevent wrinkles Rub a mixture of olive oil and the juice of a lemon into the skin before going to bed.

To soften the skin Mix together equal parts of olive oil and salt. Massage into the skin and wash off.

For weak nails Soak the nails for 5 minutes in warm olive oil and then paint the nails with white iodine.

For tired feet Massage with olive oil.

For aching muscles Massage with a mixture of olive oil and rosemary.

To clear acne Rub with a mixture of 250 ml/1 cup olive oil and 10 drops of lavender oil.

To reduce the effects of alcohol Take a couple of spoonfuls of olive oil before drinking.

For high blood pressure Boil 24 olive leaves in 250 ml/1 cup water for 15 minutes. Drink the liquid morning and night for two weeks.

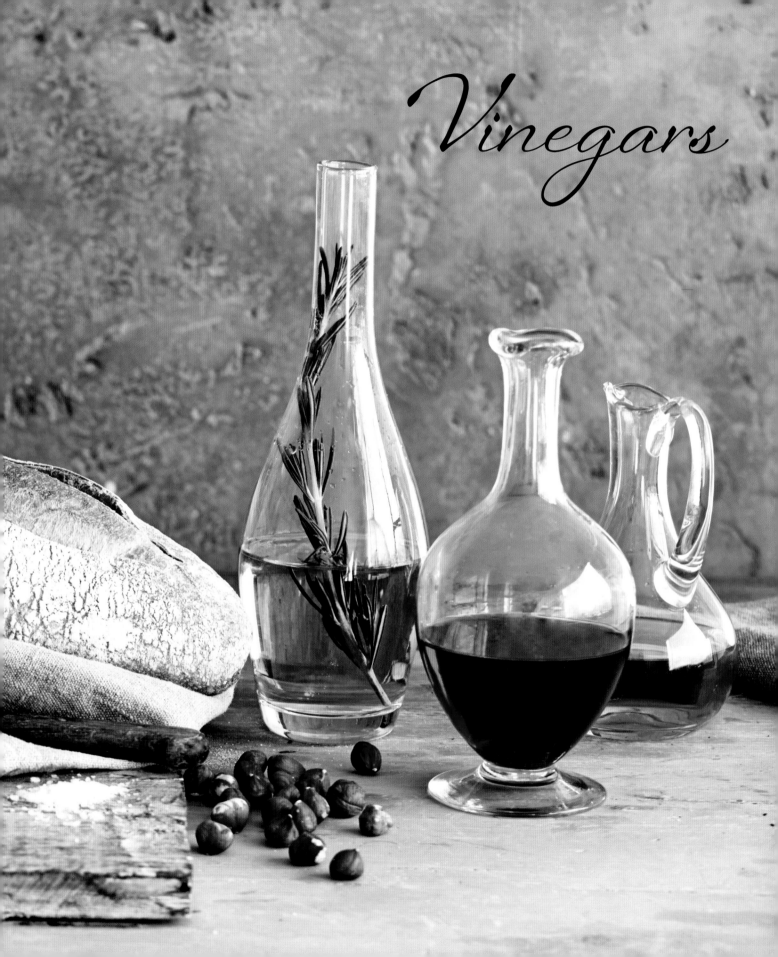

Vinegars

THIS PAGE *Levizzano Castle in autumn. The castle sits in Castelvetro di Modena, Italy, and is one of the region of Modena's most famous landmarks. You may have come across the name Modena on your bottle of balsamic vinegar. It is the only area to produce it and has PGI status (see page 57).*

Introducing vinegars

The word vinegar originates from the French, *vin aigre*, meaning 'sour wine'. Today, a variety of alcohols are used as the basis of vinegars, not just wine. Any alcoholic liquid that does not contain more than about 18% alcohol will sour if exposed to the air. Souring is caused by bacteria that attack alcohol and oxidize it to acetic acid. As they require oxygen, the bacteria grow on the surface and stick together to form a skin, known as 'vinegar plant' or 'mother of vinegar'.

Vinegar is one of the oldest ingredients in cooking and was used in Europe for thousands of years before lemon juice was even heard of. Vinegars normally contain 4–6% acetic acid, but the strength can be increased by distillation, and 'essence of vinegar' can be up to about 14%. Vinegar is commonly made by souring wine, ale (malt vinegar) or cider (cider vinegar), but vinegars are produced locally from perry, mead, rice and wine, and from fruit wines brewed with anything from currants to cashew apples.

Wine vinegar is usual in countries like France, Spain and Italy where wine is produced in quantity, but just because it is made from wine does not mean it is always good. It may be made from wine that is scarcely fit to drink, and it can be made using the quick vinegar process, in which wine is sprinkled over a container full of wood shavings (to provide a large surface) with a revolving 'sparger', a miniature version of a sewage works sprinkler. As the wine dribbles down over the shavings, it is violently attacked by the organisms that cover them, and everything is kept well oxygenated by air blown in at the bottom. In the process, quite a lot of heat is generated – the tank is maintained at 35–38°C (95–100°F), which is hot enough to drive off any of the finer and more volatile flavours.

This is why the best vinegar is still made using the old Orléans process, in which barrels are filled with a mixture of three parts wine to two parts vinegar, and inoculated with mother of vinegar and left open to allow air to enter. Establishing the vat with vinegar prevents the growth of unwanted organisms and encourages the development of vinegar organisms, which grow best in acidic conditions. In the Orléans process, the organisms slowly turn the alcohol in the wine to acid without getting hot and without losing the finer flavours of the wine. At intervals, vinegar is drawn off and more wine is added. Since this is a slow method, Orléans process vinegar is expensive, especially as the finest vinegar starts with good wine. However, the amount of vinegar used in dressing a salad ought to be small, and it is worth finding a fine wine vinegar to keep just for this purpose. The difference it makes to a salad is enormous.

The town of Modena in northern Italy produces fine wine vinegar, *aceto balsamico*, which is matured for years. It is said that it is usable after 10 years, better after 30, better still after 50 and at its best after 100 or more. It is too good to use for anything except salads.

Special types of vinegar come from particular wines, for example Sherry vinegar, which hails mainly from Jerez, Spain. Malt vinegar is essentially beer vinegar (except that the beer is not hopped) and is usually coloured brown with caramel. It is less sour than the run-of-the-mill wine vinegar, but nice flavours do not come from the fermented malt, although some aromatics may be generated by bacteria. Cider vinegar has long been popular in northeast America and in recent years has also become better known in Britain. It is supposed to be more healthy and is a basis for a few American folk medicines. However, cider vinegar has an apple juice taste that some people, including myself, do not find particularly attractive. White vinegar is as colourless as water (white wine vinegar, on the other hand, ranges from clear white to pale yellow in colour) and is used in pickles for cosmetic reasons. It can be made by decolourizing ordinary vinegar with animal charcoal or can be faked by using acetic acid and water.

Very strong vinegars, such as essence of vinegar, spirit vinegar and distilled vinegar, are used to preserve very watery vegetables or in any other situation in which ordinary vinegar will become over-diluted. These strong vinegars are made by concentrating vinegars through distillation or by diluting strong synthetic acetic acid with water.

Types of vinegar

The range of vinegars available today is vast and the one you plump for will depend largely on your taste and what you plan on using the vinegar for. It is certainly worth experimenting with less common fruit and herb vinegars. When it comes to wine and balsamic vinegars, shop around, as the quality varies enormously. Discover how to make your own vinegar on page 58.

Balsamic vinegar

Wonderfully dark and mellow, with a sweet-sour flavour, balsamic vinegar is made only in and around Modena in northern Italy (balsam simply means 'balm' and refers to the smooth, soothing character of the vinegar). There are two kinds: *industriale*, the commercial version, and *naturale*, which is still made by traditional methods in small quantities and aged for at least 15–20 years in wooden casks. There are reputed to be some exquisite vinegars that are well over 100 years old still in the possession of the families who produced them.

The vinegar is made from grape juice concentrated over a low flame and fermented slowly in a series of barrels, beginning with large chestnut or oak barrels and moving each year into progressively smaller barrels in a variety of different woods.

Balsamic vinegar is expensive, but a little goes a long way. Just a drop or two with some extra virgin olive oil makes a fine salad dressing. Do not mask the flavour with garlic and herbs or other flavours. Good mellow vinegars such as these can be surprisingly useful as a condiment to add to rich meaty soups or casseroles. Again, only a drop or two is needed. A classic dish from Modena is sliced strawberries simply sprinkled with a little balsamic vinegar and left to macerate for half an hour or so before serving.

Cider vinegar

To make cider vinegar, pure apple juice is fermented into cider, which is then exposed to the air so that it sours and is thereby converted to acetic acid, in other words vinegar. It is a clear pale brown vinegar, although unpasteurized versions can be cloudy, and the apple taste is quite strong. It is suitable for salad dressings if you like the flavour, but I find it best of all for pickling fruit – pears and plums spiced with cloves and cinnamon sticks, and the cider vinegar sweetened with a dark sugar like molasses.

Fruit vinegar

Raspberry vinegar, pear vinegar, blackcurrant vinegar, strawberry vinegar: the list of exotic new vinegars that have appeared in the last few years seems endless. However, they are not new at all. Look through any Victorian or even a much earlier cookery book and you will find a recipe for raspberry vinegar. Back then it tended to serve as the basis of a refreshing drink. Now it is used in salad dressings and particularly in sauces made from pan juices, for example when frying calves' liver or duck breasts. It also tastes very good when used as part of a basting mixture for roasting ham, duck or other fatty or rich meats.

Make fruit vinegar by steeping fresh fruit in wine vinegar and then straining it. For a more concentrated flavour, repeat this process with a second batch of fresh fruit in the same vinegar.

Herb vinegar

Subtle yet distinctive flavours can be added to salad dressings by using red or white wine vinegar in which herbs have been steeped. Tarragon vinegar is perhaps the most popular, but there is no limit to the herb-flavoured vinegars you can make. Basil vinegar, thyme vinegar, rosemary vinegar and lavender vinegar are ones I have used and enjoyed in salad dressings and in mayonnaise. Tarragon vinegar is particularly good in sauces based on eggs or butter, and is, indeed, an essential ingredient of sauce Béarnaise. It is important to use healthy, unblemished herbs, bought or picked at their peak of freshness. To make herb vinegars, simply steep a bunch of fresh herbs in wine vinegar in a sealed bottle.

Malt vinegar

Just as wine vinegar is the everyday vinegar of wine-producing areas, and rice vinegar the everyday vinegar in those areas that produce rice wine, malt vinegar is commonly used in Britain and northern Europe, the 'beer belt'. It is made from soured, unhopped beer. In its natural form the vinegar is pale and usually sold as light malt vinegar. It may be coloured brown by the addition of caramel and will sometimes be called brown malt vinegar.

In the same way that wine vinegars can be flavoured, so too can malt vinegar. It is common to find it flavoured with spices such as black and white peppercorns, allspice, cloves and tiny hot chillies/chiles. Often this is sold as pickling vinegar, since in the UK, it is malt vinegar that is usually used in the preparation of pickled onions, pickled walnuts and mixed vegetable pickles, such as piccalilli.

Use distilled malt vinegar to pickle particularly watery vegetables that are likely to dilute the vinegar. The vinegar is concentrated by distillation so that it has a higher proportion of acetic acid than the usual 4–6%. Distilled or white vinegar can also be made from other grains and is mostly used for pickling, though in Scotland it is used in the same way as ordinary malt vinegar.

On the whole, malt vinegars are best restricted to pickling and making preserves or bottled sauces such as tomato chutney. The malt flavour is too strong as a seasoning or for salad dressings. On the other hand, who could think of sprinkling wine vinegar on fish and chips? It has to be malt vinegar every time for that.

Rice vinegar

Rice vinegar is made from soured and fermented rice wine. There are rice vinegars from China that are sharp and sour, and rice vinegars from Japan that are quite different: soft, mellow, rounded, almost sweet. Indeed, if you are planning to substitute a Western vinegar (cider vinegar is the best alternative) for Japanese rice vinegar in a Japanese dish, you will need to sweeten it a little. For a really authentic flavour in Asian cooking, when making seasoned rice for sushi for example,

rice vinegar is essential. Always use Japanese rice vinegars with Japanese dishes, and Chinese rice vinegars with Chinese dishes. Fortunately, rice vinegar is also delicious in Western dishes, and makes a perfect vinaigrette with, for example, a fine nut oil.

Like other vinegars, rice vinegars are sometimes made into flavoured vinegars: with soy sauce, dashi (Japanese soup stock) or mirin (a sweet rice wine for cooking) as the base, and then additions of grated ginger for shogazu vinegar, bonito flakes for togazu vinegar, toasted sesame seeds for gomazu vinegar and chillies/chiles and onions for nanbanzu. Horseradish, mustard, citron and white radish (daikon) are also used to flavour it.

Wine vinegar

Orléans in the Loire Valley, France, is the home of the wine vinegar industry, where the traditional lengthy fermentation processes are still followed. Any vinegar made using the Orléans process, wherever it comes from, will be expensive but of superior quality.

Wine vinegar – which is the strongest natural vinegar with an acidity of about 6.5% – is made from any wine untreated with preservatives. Not surprisingly, regions that are noted for a particular wine type also produce related vinegars. Among the more readily available wine vinegars are Champagne vinegar,

malt vinegar

fruit vinegar

balsamic vinegar

cider vinegar

which is pale, light and delicate; Rioja vinegar, usually a red vinegar, which is rich, mellow and very full-bodied; and Sherry vinegar, a nutty brown vinegar matured in wooden barrels by methods similar to those used for sherry itself, and particularly full and rounded. All of these vinegars are of course especially suited to their local dishes, but are also excellent in all manner of salads. Interesting new wine vinegars are being made in other wine-making regions. For example, California produces a Zinfandel vinegar from the local grape variety.

The more expensive wine vinegars, such as Orléans vinegar and Sherry vinegar, are best used alone, but the more widely available red and white wine vinegars are the ones to use for experimenting with additional flavours.

Wine vinegars can be flavoured with fruit or herbs and also with honey, garlic, shallots, chillies/chiles, peppercorns, cloves, cinnamon, flower petals or even seaweed.

herb vinegar

red wine vinegar

white wine vinegar

Sherry vinegar

rice vinegar

Tasting notes

Wine and sherry vinegars

Valdueza: Extremadura, Spain

Blended from grapes grown on the Valdueza Estate, this vinegar is a mix of Merlot, Syrah and Cabernet Sauvignon. As elegant and refined as the Marquis who made it, Valdueza is a fresh vinegar that has just the right amount of acidity, and a delicate nuttiness that perfectly complements the estate's oils .

Don Alonso, the Marqués de Valdueza, and his son Fadrique, are serious farmers, and reflect the terroir of their hard Extremaduran land with the same commitment that their ancestors had when they popped over to South America and conquered it. They are simply determined to do things well, and if that means employing the best agronomist to help them in their choice of olive varieties and where on their farm to plant them, then so be it.

Valdespino Sherry Vinegar Reserva: Jerez, Spain

This sherry vinegar is produced in a small bodega in Jerez (which means 'Sherry' in Spanish) in Andalucia, southern Spain. They have been producing this vinegar for centuries – in fact, it dates back to 1430.

The vinegar is blended using the solera system, meaning that it uses fractional blending in such a way that the finished product is a mixture of ages. The average age gradually increases as the process lasts many years. Solera is the Spanish word for the set of barrels used in the process. The vinegar is barrel-fermented and aged, giving it a slightly sweet and well-rounded flavour, making it an excellent vinegar for red meats and bitter leaves. It has an acidity level of 7%. The vinegar originated from Sherry wine, produced from the Palomino grape, grown in a renowned vineyard, the Macharnudo Vineyard in Jerez.

A L'Olivier: Paris and Carros, France

Originally dedicated purely to olive oil, A L'Olivier was set up in 1822 by Monsieur Popelin, a former pharmacist who vaunted the oil's medicinal and culinary purposes. The shop is still on its original site in the heart of the Marais, Paris, but there are now retail outlets all over France. No longer run by the Popelin family, the business has been in the hands of the Blanvillain family since the late 1970s and attracts a loyal clientele. A L'Olivier has expanded its product range over the years, venturing beyond olive oil to traditional and fruit vinegars.

The elegant Vinaigre de Vin de Bordeaux has an acidity level of 6%. It has a rounded and well-finished flavour, which makes it extremely versatile and a must for your pantry. I love using it to deglaze lamb juices.

The Vinaigre de Vin de Reims is bolder and more intense than the Bordeaux with a higher acidity level of 7%. It has an excellent nose and balance, and partners perfectly with all green vegetables and green leaves. This vinegar has a pleasant, slightly sweet aftertaste, ideal for some of my agrodolce (sweet and sour) dishes.

Fruit vinegars

Womersley: The Cotswolds, UK

Womersley was started in 1979 by Martin and Aline Parsons at their home, Womersley Hall in Yorkshire. Mr Parsons was a keen horticulturist, and began making his fruit vinegars using produce grown in the impressive gardens of the Womersley Estate. Today, the business is run by the couple's son in the Cotswolds, and seems to be going from strength to strength, winning many awards along the way.

Made using locally sourced fruits and herbs where possible, the Womersley vinegars are wonderful ingredients to add flavour to savoury dishes, and are sweet enough to make an interesting addition to many desserts.

Use the deeply intense flavour of Blackcurrant & Rosemary with some honey as a glaze on roast duck, or to deglaze the pan after roasting a pheasant.

The hotter Golden Raspberry & Apache Chilli adds a sweet and spicy kick to scallops, while the Lemon vinegar works surprising well with Asian-inspired dishes such as a stir-fry. The Lime, Black Pepper & Lavender flavour is especially good with prawns/shrimp, and the Raspberry or the Strawberry & Mint make an average glass of Prosecco taste spectacular. Try the latter over a goat's cheese and walnut salad.

Scrubby Oak Fine Foods Ltd: King's Lynn, UK

Scrubby Oak Fine Foods Ltd was founded in 2005 by Robin and Debbie Slade with the aim of reintroducing the British public to the culinary delights of sweet English vinegars, which they had been cooking with in their own home for many years prior to launching their business.

Both Robin and Debbie are keen cooks, having been taught by their parents and grandparents how to cook using natural ingredients that are mostly home-grown or foraged from the wild. Their kitchen is home to constant experimentation with English vinegars to create new dishes and bring a fresh dimension of flavour to old favourites. Through his training in the smoking and curing industry, Robin has developed recipes that incorporate English vinegars into this process, resulting in new flavour combinations for game and fish.

English sweet vinegars were extremely popular in the Victorian kitchen, being used not only to marinate meat and fish, but to add chiefly fruit flavours to dishes when fresh fruit was out of season, and to liven up salads and winter greens. Their use as a refreshing cordial mixed with spring water was another popular one.

In launching a product that had disappeared from the UK's culinary radar for over 100 years, the Slades were taking quite a risk. However, the public was immediately impressed by the depth of flavour imparted by the vinegars and the business has been growing ever since.

These fruit vinegars have a natural intenseness of flavour and colour, coupled with a greater 'depth of body'. This is derived from the use of a mother of vinegar in the production process. A living, naturally occurring organism found in nature, this actually breaks down the fruit, root or flower ingredient used to create the desired vinegar to obtain the sugars it needs to grow, converting the raw ingredient to vinegar in the process. The process is not quick, and can take anything from several months to four years, depending on the type of vinegar being 'grown'.

These vinegars work well in a range of marinades and salad dressings. However, this is by no means the limit of their culinary use. Tasty soft cheese and yoghurt dips may be quickly whipped up by adding a few drops of the vinegar of choice to them, best served chilled. Add to stews and casseroles, or use as a garnish for meat or fish dishes or as a cure for fish to be eaten raw. They may even be used in meringue and pavlova recipes and sweet sponge cakes, or simply drizzled over sorbets, pancakes or ice cream. The list is virtually endless with new uses being discovered all the time. Happy inventing!

Balsamic vinegars

La Vecchia Dispensa Red Label: Castelvetro, Italy

The little town of Castelvetro is set on one of the first lines of hills that sweep up from the plain of the River Po, and carry on to become the towering Apennine mountain range. It was here that the Pelloni family had a beautiful restaurant bordering the chequerboard square; Mrs Pelloni cooked, Mr Pelloni chatted to diners including the executives from the nearby Ferrari factory in Marinello (and other guests), and their daughter Roberta completed the picture as the waitress.

One day, down from the snowy mountains came a handsome young ski instructor named Marino, who fell into the arms of Roberta. But was Marino going to be accepted into the family? Not until he learned how to make balsamic vinegar, which he did over many years under the tutelage of his by-then father-in-law.

The family make wonderful balsamic vinegar in the traditional way. Their attention to detail is reflected in the superb quality of their products and the care that they take to produce them. The grapes that produce the oil must come from local producers, and the barrels used in the fermentation process have been in the family for generations. Red Label Balsamic Vinegar used to be called '8 Year Old' before the new, stricter Protected Geographical Indication (PGI) regulations came in. Rich and complex, with a lovely sweetness imparted from the wooden barrels it has been aged in, the texture of this balsamic vinegar is dense enough to be used in dressing salads as well as in cooking.

Try mixing this vinegar with Colonna Lemon Oil (see page 33), and using the blend as a dip for bread or to drizzle over some new-season asparagus served with slithers of Parmesan. It also makes a great base for a rich gravy to serve alongside roasted meats. This vinegar is the one used in the River Café's recipe for Lamb Shanks in Balsamic Vinegar.

Aspall Apple Balsamic Vinegar: Suffolk, UK

I was rather reluctant to try this vinegar, but its recommendation came from a reliable source. I was conscious of Aspall's ciders; indeed, the producer's name is practically synonymous with cider in the UK. Aspall has been producing cider since the mid-eighteenth century and has since expanded its repertoire to apple juice and vinegar. While I do like their ciders, I was worried that their Apple Balsamic Vinegar was a bridge too far. However, I was pleasantly surprised and can now see why it picked up a Great Taste Gold award. This vinegar is fresh and lively, excellent with spices, fabulous in drinks and a good all-round vinegar to enjoy alongside a wide range of flavours. It has a lovely rich caramel colour too, making it a great addition to your store cupboard.

Acetum Aceto Balsamico: Modena, Italy

Produced in Modena, the home of balsamic vinegar, this vinegar has an acidity level of 6%. It has been produced using grape must with the addition of wine vinegar. This dilutes the flavour, but it is balanced and extremely pleasant. It has a syrupy viscosity, and I would enjoy this over ice cream and with bitter leaves such as chicory/Belgian endive, rocket/arugula and watercress.

Making vinegars

Vinegar is very easily made at home by putting wine (including homemade wine) or any other alcoholic liquid into a container, preferably one with a tap/faucet at the bottom, and by adding mother of vinegar (a fermenting bacteria composed of cellulose and acetic acid bacteria) to act as a 'starter' (a culture used to instigate souring). A skin of mother of vinegar will shortly form over the wine. If this later becomes too white and thick, the top layer should be removed, as it may prevent air from getting to the harmless bacteria beneath. The underlying pink skin should be left. When it is ready, some of the vinegar can be run off (or siphoned off from the bottom if it is in a vessel with no tap/faucet) and more wine added. Vinegar exposed to the air will lose strength because of bacteria that attack the acetic acid, so vinegar bottles should be well filled and corked.

In the past, it was quite usual for cooks to make sugar vinegar, something that can be done quite simply as follows: boil a suitable volume of water and add sugar at the rate of 150 g/5½ oz. per 1 litre/quart. You can add brown sugar or molasses for flavour, if you like. Traditionally, the liquid, when cool, was put in a not-quite-full cask and a piece of toast covered in yeast was floated on top. A piece of brown paper was pasted over the bung hole and well pricked with a skewer to let in air. A barrel of sugar and water, if put down in April, would be vinegar ready for bottling by September. It would be ready quicker if mother of vinegar was added, though.

Old directions for making mother of vinegar are to put 100 g/3½ oz. sugar and 225 g/8 oz. treacle/molasses in 3.5 litres/quarts water and bring to the boil, then cool, cover and leave in a warm place for 6 weeks. If all goes well, mother of vinegar will form on top and can be used as a starter. Homemade vinegar is best pasteurized or brought almost to the boil before bottling.

Vinegar is often flavoured with various herbs and aromatics, the best-known varieties being tarragon, chilli/chile and garlic vinegars, but cucumber, basil, rose, violet, celery (with celery seed), cress or mustard (also with seed) and shallot vinegars are also made. To make any of these, it is necessary only to infuse the flavourings in a bottle of vinegar for some days. It used to be popular to make vinegars with quite complicated mixtures of herbs, garlic, onion and spices, which were essentially bottled sauces. Sweet fruit vinegars (such as raspberry, currant and gooseberry) were made for diluting and used in refreshing summer drinks, but these have also fallen out of fashion.

Due to its acetic acid content, vinegar is a preservative, which is why it is used in pickles and chutneys. As vinegars vary, it is sometimes best to dilute them with a little water and not to slavishly follow recipes with full-strength products. Tiny amounts of vinegar can improve some surprising things (yoghurt and strawberries are examples).

Yamabukusu is a Japanese sweet vinegar, used for seasoning rice. You can quickly make your own version by adding 3 tablespoons sugar, 3 teaspoons salt and a pinch of monosodium glutamate to 250 ml/1 cup vinegar.

OPPOSITE *Once you have mastered making your own vinegar, you can experiment with different flavours. Garlic, fresh red chilli/chile and tarragon are all perfect companions. It is worth making a wide range to use in different recipes.*

Recipes

Appetizers

Carpaccio with Gorgonzola and walnuts

This is my improvisation on the classic recipe and is very easy to prepare. Be sure to use prime ingredients, particularly when it comes to the beef.

750 g/1 lb. 10 oz. beef fillet, tail end in one piece

200 g/7 oz. rocket/arugula

200 g/7 oz. aged Gorgonzola Piccante, crumbled

85 g/⅔ cup fresh coarsely chopped walnuts

a handful of fresh flat-leaf parsley, roughly chopped

4–6 tablespoons fruity extra virgin olive oil

sea salt and freshly ground black pepper

2 unwaxed lemons, halved, to serve

Serves 4

Wrap the beef in clingfilm/plastic wrap and place in the freezer for 2 hours (this makes it easier to slice). Remove the plastic and, using a sharp filleting knife, cut the beef into paper-thin slices.

Cover four individual plates with the carpaccio slices. Rinse the rocket/arugula and place a mound on top. Sprinkle with the cheese, walnuts and parsley. Drizzle with the oil and season. Serve with the lemon halves for squeezing over.

Asian-style salt and pepper prawns

4 tablespoons/¼ cup
cornflour/cornstarch

4 teaspoons sea salt

2 teaspoons freshly ground
black pepper

1½ teaspoons Chinese five-spice
powder

1 kg/2¼ lbs. raw king prawns/
jumbo shrimp, peeled and deveined

150 ml/⅔ cup sunflower or
groundnut/peanut oil

1 medium fresh red chilli/chile

20 g/a handful of fresh coriander/
cilantro or flat-leaf parsley, to garnish

1 unwaxed lemon, cut into thick
slices, to serve

Serves 4–6

Deliciously straightforward, this makes a super starter for informal suppers.

Mix the cornflour/cornstarch, salt, pepper and five-spice on a large plate. Dust the prawns/shrimp in the seasoned cornflour/cornstarch and shake off any excess.

Place a wok or similar vessel on a medium-high heat, add the oil and heat until smoking.

Fry the prawns/shrimp in batches for about 2 minutes until golden and crisp, turning halfway through cooking. Drain the prawns/shrimp on paper towels and keep them warm.

Fry the chilli/chile for a few seconds after you have cooked the prawns/shrimp.

Serve with the fried chilli/chile and lemon slices, garnished with the coriander/cilantro or parsley, and more seasoning if you like.

Homemade za'atar

4 teaspoons sesame seeds

4 teaspoons cumin seeds

2 tablespoons dried thyme

4 teaspoons sumac

2 teaspoons sea salt

Makes
1 x 150-g / 5-oz. jar

This spice is used frequently in Lebanese food. It is wonderful with bread or on fish or meat, as a condiment or mixed into Greek yoghurt. You can even add it to scrambled eggs, steak and more.

Toast the sesame seeds and cumin on a medium heat in a small pan for 2 minutes until they are lightly toasted.

Combine all the ingredients together and grind either in a pestle and mortar or in a food processor until finely mixed. Store in an airtight jar.

Add some high quality extra virgin olive oil to make a dip for bread.

Roman artichokes

Artichokes grow all over Italy, but the Lazio region, and Rome in particular, is especially renowned for its small, tender artichokes. Speciality dishes feature on restaurant menus throughout the capital during artichoke season. Try to buy young artichokes with long stalks, as these are tender and won't yet have developed much in the way of a choke. For this appetizer, the artichokes are best served warm.

4 medium globe artichokes

1 unwaxed lemon, halved

3 bay leaves

150 ml/⅔ cup dry white wine

FOR THE DRESSING:

a large handful of fresh mint, finely chopped

2 garlic cloves, finely chopped

3–4 tablespoons extra virgin olive oil

2 tablespoons white wine vinegar

sea salt and freshly ground black pepper

Serves 4

Prepare the artichokes one at a time. Trim the base of the stalk at an angle, then peel the stem. Cut off the leaves about ½ cm/¼ in. from the top. Rub the cut surfaces with a lemon half. Now start peeling away the artichoke leaves, removing at least four layers, until the leaves begin to look pale. Spread the top leaves and use a teaspoon to scrape out the choke. Immerse the artichoke in a bowl of cold water with the other lemon half added (to prevent discolouration). Repeat to prepare the rest of the artichokes.

Place the bay leaves, lemon halves, wine and artichokes in a large saucepan and add enough cold water to cover (the artichokes should fit snugly in the pan). Bring to the boil, cover and simmer for about 30–35 minutes until the artichokes are tender. Drain the artichokes thoroughly.

To make the dressing, place the chopped mint leaves and garlic in a bowl with the oil and vinegar. Season to taste and whisk thoroughly to blend.

Arrange the artichokes upside down (with their stalks sticking up) on serving plates. Pour the dressing over the warm artichokes and serve.

6 (bell) peppers, a mixture of red, yellow and orange

3 tablespoons white wine vinegar

6 tablespoons fruity extra virgin olive oil, Ligurian if possible

50 g/⅓ cup sultanas/golden raisins

1½ teaspoons cumin seeds

1 teaspoon crushed dried peperoncini chillies/chiles

sea salt and freshly ground black pepper

1 garlic clove, finely sliced

2 teaspoons caster/granulated sugar

FOR THE SALAD:

3 x 125 g/4½ oz. balls buffalo mozzarella, sliced

6 Queen Spanish or other large green olives, stoned and sliced lengthways

60 g/2¼ oz. rocket/arugula

1 tablespoon extra virgin olive oil, light and not too bold

TO SERVE:

crusty bread for mopping up juices

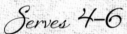

Serves 4–6

Sweet and sour peppers with mozzarella

This antipasto is timeless and its colour, simplicity and flavour always hit the right key. It is ideal for those with busy lives, as it can be made days in advance. There was always some roasted pepper in my Nonna's kitchen to dip crusty bread into as a wonderful snack.

Preheat the oven to 200°C (400°F) Gas 6.

Place the peppers on a baking sheet lined with baking parchment and bake for 25 minutes until slightly blackened and deflated. Leave to cool. Peel the peppers and discard the seeds, then cut into 1-cm/½-in. strips.

Mix the pepper strips with the vinegar, oil, sultanas/golden raisins, cumin and peperoncini chillies/chiles. Season to taste. Add the garlic and sugar and leave to infuse.

To serve, divide the mozzarella between 4–6 plates, spoon over the pepper mixture and scatter over the olives. Toss the rocket/arugula leaves in the oil and scatter some on each plate. Serve immediately.

Pickled lox

300 ml/1¼ cups distilled white vinegar

125 g/⅔ cup light brown sugar

25 g/2 tablespoons sea salt

6 fresh bay leaves

2 teaspoons coriander seeds

2 teaspoons yellow mustard seeds

1 teaspoon black peppercorns

1 teaspoon allspice berries

20 g/a handful of fresh dill, chopped, plus extra to garnish

500 g/1 lb. salmon fillet, skin on

1 white onion, finely chopped, optional

TO SERVE:

rye bread

cream cheese

Serves 8

This recipe is in honour of my friends in Ukraine. The chefs that I have worked with over there are very proud of their national dishes; this recipe is a close cousin of one of these national dishes, and I hope you will return to it frequently for its ease, flavour and wow factor.

Put all the ingredients except the salmon and onion into a non-reactive saucepan with 1 litre/1 quart water and bring to the boil. Turn down the heat and simmer for 5 minutes. Leave to cool to room temperature.

Put the salmon in a non-reactive container and pour over the brine. Cover lightly. Put into the fridge and leave for 3 days.

Take out the salmon and cut into thin slices (like smoked salmon), removing and discarding the skin. Put the slices in a shallow bowl with the chopped onion, if using, and about 100 ml/½ cup of the brine. Serve with rye bread and cream cheese, garnished with dill.

Pickled red onions

225 ml/1 cup olive oil

1.5 kg/3¼ lbs. red onions, thinly sliced

225 g/1⅓ cups stoned/pitted prunes, coarsely chopped

200 ml/¾ cup red wine

350 g/1¾ cups demerara/raw brown sugar

250 ml/1 cup Sherry vinegar

1 tablespoon sea salt

1 tablespoon freshly ground black pepper

1½ teaspoons ground allspice

Makes
6 x 350-g/12-oz. jars

This is another all-time favourite of mine. The rich colour of the onions in their spiced vinegar makes me think of glistening jewels. They are good in sandwiches, served with cheese or spring vegetables. I always have a jar of these in my cupboard.

Heat the oil in a frying pan/skillet, add the onions and cook them over a high heat for 5–6 minutes, stirring all the time, until softened. Reduce the heat and simmer for 40 minutes.

Add the prunes and red wine to the pan. Cook over a high heat until most of the liquid has evaporated. Then add the sugar and vinegar and reduce the heat again. Simmer the mixture until it thickens.

Remove from the heat and add the salt, pepper and the allspice. Leave the onions to cool before sealing them in hot, sterilized jars. Store them in a cool, dry, dark place.

Dried tomatoes stuffed with anchovies and capers

2 kg/4½ lbs. good plum tomatoes (smell the stalk end for a peppery scent)

75 g/½ cup salted capers, rinsed at least twice and finely chopped

75 g/2¾ oz. anchovy fillets, finely chopped

4 dried chillies/chiles (peperoncini), or more to taste

6 garlic cloves, blanched briefly in boiling water and finely chopped

extra virgin olive oil (from Puglia if possible) to fill the jars

Makes
6 x 350-g/12-oz. jars

Tomatoes can become a problem in Italy, but only because we have so many that all seem to ripen at the same time! The best tomato for southern Italians is undisputedly the San Marzano tomato – the tomato with attitude. It has a great flavour for sauces and also this preserve, which brings back a rush of childhood memories, possibly stronger than any other dish in the book.

Preheat the oven to 140°C (275°F) Gas 1.

Pour water into a pan large enough to hold all the tomatoes at the same time, and bring to the boil. Add the tomatoes when the water is boiling. Just a couple of minutes is enough to soften the skins slightly.

Drain the tomatoes, then cut them in half and spread out on a baking sheet. Place in the preheated oven for an hour, or alternatively, let them dry in the sun.

In the meantime, prepare the seasoning by mixing the capers, anchovies, chillies/chiles and garlic together.

Take one half of the tomato and sprinkle with the seasoning mixture, then place the other half on top, kissing like a sandwich. Place the tomatoes on the bottom of a hot, sterilized jar one after the other until you reach the top. Cover with extra virgin olive oil, then seal and refrigerate. Enjoy in the winter.

1 medium pumpkin, weighing about 1 kg/2¼ lbs.

sea salt

2 garlic cloves, blanched briefly in boiling water and roughly chopped

225 ml/1 cup extra virgin olive oil

50 ml/3 tablespoons white wine vinegar

2 teaspoons dried thyme

Makes 1x 450-g/1-lb. jar

Pickled pumpkin

I first encountered this delicacy in southern Italy. It is quite special and easy to make. Enjoy this pickled pumpkin in sandwiches and salads and as an accompaniment.

Using a sharp knife, cut the pumpkin in half and scoop out the seeds. Cut into sections, remove the peel and chop the flesh into small cubes.

Bring a large saucepan of salted water to the boil. Add the pumpkin flesh and boil for 4 minutes, until tender but firm (it should still have a little bite in it). Drain, put in a large bowl and leave to cool.

When cold, add the garlic to the pumpkin with the oil, vinegar and thyme. Mix well together, then pack in a hot, sterilized jar and cover. Store in a cool, dry, dark place.

Pickled aubergines

2 medium aubergines/eggplant

sea salt

2–3 teaspoons dried oregano

1 tablespoon white wine vinegar

2 garlic cloves, peeled

225 ml/1 cup extra virgin olive oil

Makes
1 x 500-g/1-lb. 2-oz. jar

This is a Nonna Ferrigno recipe that makes a wonderful gift. It's utterly delicious with sourdough bread as a *merenda* (snack), or antipasto selection.

Slice the aubergines/eggplant into thin, short strips. Put in a colander and sprinkle with salt. Place a plate on top and weigh it down. Leave for 30 minutes to extract the bitter juices from the aubergine/eggplant.

Rinse the aubergine/eggplant well and put in a saucepan of boiling salted water. Boil for 4 minutes. Drain and leave to cool.

When cold, add all the remaining ingredients to the aubergine/eggplant and mix together.

Pack in a hot, sterilized jar and seal. Refrigerate and leave for a month before use.

Bruschetta with caramelized red onion and young Pecorino

3 tablespoons fruity extra virgin olive oil, plus extra for serving

3 red onions, chopped

2 bay leaves

a sprig of fresh rosemary, leaves picked

2 tablespoons balsamic vinegar

55 g/¼ cup packed soft brown sugar

4 slices of country bread, open textured, with a firm crust

4 handfuls of pea shoots

sea salt and freshly ground black pepper

125 g/4½ oz. young Pecorino cheese

Serves 4

This recipe celebrates young Pecorino, which is gloriously sweet, and goes magnificently with the acidity of the onion marmalade. I enjoyed it at La Buca di San Petronio, a modern trattoria in central Bologna run by a young couple, Giorgio and Antonia Fini. I loved it, as well as the incredibly memorable pasta served with four wild herbs that followed.

Heat 2 tablespoons of the olive oil, then add the onions, bay leaves and rosemary. Brown the onions well over a low-to-medium heat, stirring regularly. Add the vinegar and stir well. Add the sugar and cook over a low heat for 30 minutes. The mixture should be thick, shiny and rich red. Leave to cool.

Heat a ridged cast-iron griddle/grill pan until hot. Add the bread slices and cook for 1–2 minutes on each side, until lightly toasted and charred at the edges. Put the pea shoots in a bowl, add the remaining tablespoon of olive oil and season to taste. Toss to combine.

To serve, spread 1 tablespoon of the red onion mixture on each piece of toast and put on serving plates. Add a handful of pea shoots and crumble the Pecorino on top. Sprinkle with more olive oil and pepper and serve.

Salads and soups

Tomato and mint salad

I remember this salad from a business trip in Sicily where family friends were kind enough to serve it for lunch. The taste of the salad reflects the region's Byzantine flavour, typified by the mint, which releases a special flavour when blended with red onions. Be discerning when choosing tomatoes. I often find cherry tomatoes on the vine have a reliably good flavour compared to other varieties. Buy them when they're firm and bright in colour. In Italy, Spain and France you can buy your tomatoes in so many different degrees of ripeness. You will often be asked if you want to eat them that day, the next day or use them to make a sauce. I really enjoy being allowed to choose the different tomatoes. To pick the best ones, smell the stalk end – they should smell peppery.

4 firm, bright red tomatoes

½ a small red onion

a handful of fresh mint

sea salt and freshly ground black pepper

2 tablespoons fruity extra virgin olive oil

1 tablespoon balsamic vinegar

25 g/1 oz. freshly grated Parmesan shavings

TO SERVE:

crusty or French bread

Serves 4

Cut the tomatoes into slices and slice the onion into rings. Roughly chop the mint.

Arrange the tomatoes and onions on a serving plate before adding the mint.

Season to taste, then pour over the olive oil and balsamic vinegar. Sprinkle over the Parmesan shavings and serve with bread.

Fennel and celery salad

2 medium fennel bulbs, stalks discarded

6 pale inner celery stalks/ribs, leaves discarded and thinly sliced

250-g/8-oz. ball buffalo mozzarella, torn

½ tablespoon grated lemon zest (preferably from an unwaxed organic lemon)

2 tablespoons freshly squeezed lemon juice

6 tablespoons fruity extra virgin olive oil

¼ teaspoon fine sea salt

Serves 6

The inner stalks of celery and fennel, plus soft chunks of mozzarella create a clean, cool and striking salad. The Italian name for the dish – Dama Bianca – which refers to a 'woman in white', alludes to its pale hues.

Halve the fennel lengthways, then thinly slice crosswise about ½ cm/ ¼ in. thick. Toss with the celery and arrange on a platter with the torn mozzarella.

Whisk together the lemon zest, juice, oil and sea salt. Drizzle the dressing over the salad.

Broad bean and pea salad with sourdough croutons and tarragon

This salad is full of summer promise and is made all the better if the vegetables come from your garden. It is one of my favourites. Why not make your own bread to serve alongside it?

250 g/9 oz. podded broad/fava beans or butter/lima beans

200 g/7 oz. podded fresh garden peas/English peas

3 slices of sourdough bread, ideally a little dry

1–2 tablespoons olive oil

4 tablespoons crème fraîche or sour cream

2 teaspoons Dijon mustard

grated zest and juice of 1 unwaxed lemon

1 garlic clove, crushed

sea salt and freshly ground black pepper

100 ml/6 tablespoons fruity extra virgin olive oil, plus extra for drizzling

40 g/⅓ cup freshly grated Parmesan cheese, plus extra shavings for scattering

2 generous handfuls of fresh tarragon, chopped, plus extra leaves for scattering

2 Little Gem lettuces or several handfuls of Cos/Romaine lettuce

Serves 4–6

Bring the water to the boil in a medium-sized saucepan. Add some salt and the beans and cook them for 5 minutes. Refresh the beans with cold water, drain them well and remove the skins to reveal their vibrant green flesh.

If the peas are young and sweet, they can be served raw. If not, cook them for 3 minutes in boiling water, then refresh in cold water to prevent them cooking further.

Cut the bread into fork-friendly squares and heat the olive oil in a frying pan/skillet. Fry until golden, then put aside.

Combine the crème fraîche or sour cream with the mustard, lemon zest and juice and garlic, season with salt and pepper and slowly add the extra virgin olive oil until you have a thick, unctuous dressing. Add the grated Parmesan cheese. The thickness of the dressing should be that of double/heavy cream. Add water to slacken it if necessary.

Add the chopped tarragon to the dressing. Tear the lettuce and toss with the beans, peas, dressing and half the croutons.

Scatter with the remaining croutons, tarragon leaves and Parmesan shavings. Drizzle the salad with a little more of the extra virgin olive oil before serving.

Pea shoot, endive, Provolone, pear and walnut salad

Provolone is a cow's milk cheese from Italy's southern region. It has a slightly smoky flavour and fine texture. The colour is pale yellow when aged between 2 and 3 months, but as the cheese ripens, the colour and flavour deepen. A mature goat's cheese would also work very well.

100 g/1 cup fresh walnut halves

1 head chicory/Belgian endive

½ head radicchio

a handful of fresh basil, torn

a handful of mint, chopped

125 g/4½ oz. pea shoots

2 large, ripe but firm pears (Williams are good)

150 g/5½ oz. Provolone cheese, cut into triangles

FOR THE VINAIGRETTE:

1 tablespoon red wine vinegar

2 teaspoons aged balsamic vinegar

3 tablespoons walnut oil

1 tablespoon olive oil

sea salt and freshly ground black pepper

Serves 4–6

Preheat the oven to 180°C (350°F) Gas 4. Spread the walnuts on a baking sheet and bake them for 10 minutes until they are fragrant. Let cool before roughly chopping.

Next, make the vinaigrette. Combine the salt, red wine vinegar and balsamic vinegar in a bowl and whisk until the salt has dissolved. Trickle in the two types of oil, whisking all the while until the mixture has emulsified. Season to taste with pepper.

Separate the chicory/endive and radicchio leaves, rinse well and pat dry. Place in a bowl with the herbs and pea shoots. Add 2 tablespoons of the vinaigrette and toss well, then use to make a bed on a plate.

Quarter and core the pears, then arrange them on top of the leaves with the cheese and walnuts. Drizzle with the dressing and serve straight away.

30 g/¼ cup pumpkin seeds

6 tablespoons tamari soy sauce

4 medium organic carrots,
cut into matchsticks

150 g/5½ oz. pea shoots

3 spring onions/scallions,
sliced at an angle

FOR THE GINGER DRESSING:

1 cm/½ in. fresh ginger, peeled
and grated

2 tablespoons mirin
(sweetened rice wine)

1 tablespoon rice vinegar

2 tablespoons toasted sesame oil

sea salt and freshly ground
black pepper

Serves 4–6

Asian-style carrot salad with ginger dressing and pumpkin seeds

This salad is full of history for me. As a very young cookery teacher, I used to demonstrate this dish regularly. I love its colours and crunch factor. Providing your store cupboard is well stocked, this salad can be made quickly and easily.

Dry-fry the pumpkin seeds in a medium-sized frying pan/skillet and constantly toss the pan to prevent the seeds from burning. Once they start to colour, turn off the heat, add 4 tablespoons of the tamari and stir to combine. Leave them to cool and go crunchy.

Now make the dressing. Combine the ingredients in a jam jar with a lid. Season with salt and pepper. Shake well and set aside until needed. The dressing will store very well in the fridge.

Combine the carrots, pea shoots and spring onions/scallions. Sprinkle over the crunchy pumpkin seeds. Shake the dressing, pour it over the salad and serve at once.

Farro and bean soup

Barley-like and light brown in colour, farro has recently been rediscovered and is now valued both for its taste and nutritional value. Farro is cultivated almost exclusively in the Garfagnana, the mountainous region of Tuscany, and its use has brought a fresh recognition to Tuscan cooking. This soup is typical of Garfagnana.

250 g/9 oz. dried borlotti beans, soaked overnight, drained and rinsed

2 medium white onions, finely chopped

5 fresh sage leaves

3 garlic cloves

4 tablespoons/¼ cup olive oil

1 medium red onion, finely chopped

2 carrots, diced

2–4 celery sticks/ribs, diced

a handful of fresh flat-leaf parsley

275 g/9½ oz. canned Italian plum tomatoes and their liquid

200 g/1¼ cups farro, soaked overnight, drained and rinsed

sea salt and freshly ground black pepper

6 tablespoons estate-bottled extra virgin olive oil

Serves 8

Place the beans in a large saucepan with one onion, half the sage, one of the garlic cloves and enough water to cover by at least 5 cm/2 in.

Cover and cook for 1 hour or until tender. When the beans are cooked, pass the contents of the pan through either a food processor or a vegetable mill.

Heat the oil in a large saucepan. Add the red and remaining white onion, the carrots, celery, most of the parsley, remaining garlic and sage leaves, the tomatoes and 3 tablespoons hot water and continue to cook for 10 minutes.

Add the farro and simmer on a low heat for around 30 minutes until tender. Add salt and pepper to taste and the bean mixture. Stir and warm through until hot. Adjust the seasoning, if necessary, and serve with drizzlings of the extra virgin olive oil and the remaining parsley.

Cook's note: A relation of wheat, farro is an ancient grain that was originally cultivated and eaten by the Assyrians, Egyptians and Romans. The latter boiled the kernels in a stew and used the flour in a type of polenta. Farro is planted in autumn on graduated terraces, rather like rice. However, it does not like 'standing' in water like rice, which is why it does so well in mountainous country. The grain is resistant to disease and therefore needs no fungicides or pesticides, so it is totally organic. It is harvested in June: the stalks are cut from the fields and allowed to dry for a few months before being beaten to remove the kernels. There are two types of farro: the grain farro and *Triticum spelta*, also called farricello or spelt. The difference between the two types is that farro needs a 12-hour soaking period, while spelt can be cooked without soaking beforehand.

Leek and tomato soup with crusty bread and basil

I am hungrily eyeing the leeks growing at the moment in my garden. Picking them young and tender is the secret to this totally memorable soup. I love the mixture of the humblest of ingredients married together, relying on an exceptional oil for a total taste sensation.

6 baby leeks

3 tablespoons olive oil

750 g/1 lb. 10 oz. fresh, ripe tomatoes

sea salt and freshly ground black pepper

½ teaspoon crushed dried peperoncini chillies/chiles

450 g/1 lb. crusty day-old bread

750 ml/3 cups vegetable stock

6 fresh basil leaves

12 teaspoons extra virgin olive oil

Serves 6

Slice the leeks and wash them well under cold running water.

Heat the olive oil in a large saucepan and add the leeks. Fry them for 10 minutes.

Purée the tomatoes in a blender or food processor and add them to the leeks. Add salt and pepper to taste, together with the peperoncini chillies/chiles. Simmer for 30 minutes.

Cut the bread into small pieces and add it to the pan. Combine well, and lightly cook for 5 minutes. Add the stock, mix well and simmer for a further 10 minutes.

Serve in individual bowls. Add a basil leaf and 2 teaspoons extra virgin olive oil to each serving.

Pasta and lighter bites

Potato gnocchi with truffle oil and sage

Gnocchi should be feather-light and airy, and the use of a floury potato is essential for great results. The varieties that I recommend are Rooster, King Edward, Pentland Crown and American Russet. Baking the potatoes achieves great results. I think it is slightly easier too, plus you get a really great flavour from the baked potato, which has a distinctive nutty taste close to the skin.

750 g/1 lb. 10 oz. even-sized floury old potatoes

150 g/1 cup plus 3 tablespoons Italian '00' flour

1 teaspoon fine sea salt

1 teaspoon white/black truffle paste, optional

1 large egg, lightly beaten

75g/5 tablespoons unsalted butter

a handful of large fresh sage leaves

1 tablespoon truffle-infused olive oil

fresh truffle shavings, optional

TO SERVE:

75 g/¾ cup freshly grated Parmesan cheese

Serves 4–6

Preheat the oven to 200°C (400°F) Gas 6. Place the potatoes on a baking sheet lined with baking parchment and bake for 40–45 minutes. If the potatoes are tender, they are cooked.

Leave to cool slightly. Cut the potatoes in half and scoop out the flesh. Place the flesh in a ricer or Mouli grater and process directly onto the work surface. Scatter the flour around the riced potatoes, make a well in the centre and add the salt, truffle paste, if using, and the egg. Mix gently until you have a soft dough. Add more flour as needed, taking care not to overwork the dough. Shape it into long, narrow logs. Wrap each log in clingfilm/plastic wrap and leave to rest for 10 minutes.

Slowly melt the butter in a pan over a low heat. Add the sage.

Roll the dough into a narrow sausage, 1 cm/½ in. thick. Cut the log into short 2 cm/¾ in. pieces and pinch the gnocchi to create texture for the sauce. You may like to roll the gnocchi over the back of the tines of a fork. Set aside on a floured tray and keep covered.

Bring a large pan of salted water to a rolling boil and drop in the gnocchi in batches. When the gnocchi rise to the surface, count to 30, remove the gnocchi and add them to the warm butter. Add the truffle oil, truffle shavings, if using, and Parmesan cheese, then serve.

Spaghetti with oven-roasted tomatoes, thyme and peppered Pecorino

This is a simple but flavoursome recipe that can be prepared in several ways. The common denominator is fresh lemon thyme, which helps blend the tomatoes with the peppery, spicy taste of the Pecorino. In the winter use oven-roasted tomatoes because they are more savoury, but during the summer months try using fresh ones if you can.

400 g/14 oz. ripe cherry tomatoes on the vine (smell the stalk end for a peppery scent)

4 teaspoons fresh lemon thyme, finely chopped

2 garlic cloves, finely chopped

6 tablespoons olive, grapeseed or groundnut/peanut oil

a handful of fresh basil leaves, torn

sea salt and freshly ground black pepper

400 g/14 oz. dried spaghetti

90 g/3¼ oz. peppered/regular Pecorino shavings

3 tablespoons estate-bottled extra virgin olive oil

Serves 4

Preheat the oven to 150°C (300°F) Gas 2.

Place the tomatoes on a baking sheet, cut-sides up. Sprinkle with the thyme, garlic and half of the oil, and roast in the oven for 1 hour. Leave to cool.

Heat the remaining oil in a large, deep-sided frying pan/skillet over a low heat and add the tomatoes and basil. Season with salt and pepper.

Cook the pasta in abundant boiling salted water until al dente. Drain well. Transfer the pasta to the tomatoes in the pan. Add the Pecorino shavings and extra virgin olive oil, toss and serve immediately.

Linguine with prawns

On a taxi journey from High Street Kensington in Central London to Leiths School of Food and Wine recently, I fell into a conversation with the taxi driver about this recipe and the many ways of making it. I hope you like my version. Some cooks add tomatoes, while some add more chilli and others don't add chilli at all.

2 tablespoons olive, groundnut/peanut, rapeseed/canola or grapeseed oil

1 medium onion or 2 shallots, finely chopped

1 garlic clove, finely chopped

a handful of fresh flat-leaf parsley, chopped

1 medium fresh red chilli/chile, deseeded and finely chopped

500 g/1 lb. 2 oz. raw king prawns/jumbo shrimp, peeled and deveined

sea salt and freshly ground black pepper

400 g/14 oz. linguine pasta

3 tablespoons light Ligurian extra virgin olive oil

Serves 4–6

Heat the oil in a large, deep-sided frying pan/skillet. Add the onion or shallots, garlic and 4 tablespoons water. Cook over a medium heat for 10 minutes until the water has almost entirely evaporated.

Add the parsley, chilli/chile and prawns/shrimp, along with salt and pepper to taste. Simmer with a little more water if necessary for 8 minutes until the prawns/shrimp turn pink.

Meanwhile, bring a large pan of salted water to the boil and cook the linguine until al dente, stirring often. Drain the pasta and add to the prawns/shrimp. Stir well, season with the extra virgin olive oil and salt and pepper and serve immediately.

Orecchiette with chickpeas

You can barely take a step in Puglia without encountering homemade orecchiette (Italian for 'little ear'), which have an unusual hybrid flavour somewhere between dried and fresh pasta (they're made from semolina and contain no eggs). They are an ideal shape to pair with chickpeas.

FOR THE SAUCE:

100 g/3½ oz. dried chickpeas

2 garlic cloves, left whole, plus 4 garlic cloves, finely chopped

3 bay leaves

150 ml/⅔ cup olive oil

1 medium onion, finely chopped

2 celery stalks/ribs, finely chopped

2 medium carrots, finely chopped

¼ to ½ teaspoon crushed, dried peperoncini chillies/chiles

1 teaspoon fine sea salt

350 g/12 oz. vine-ripened tomatoes, finely chopped

a handful of fresh flat-leaf parsley, finely chopped

FOR THE ORECCHIETTE:

¾ teaspoon fine sea salt

225 g/1¾ cups semolina, plus extra for sprinkling

grated Pecorino or Parmesan cheese, to serve

Serves 8

Soak the dried chickpeas in water to cover by 5 cm/2 in. overnight (8 hours), then drain (or use canned chickpeas – see cook's notes below).

Simmer the soaked chickpeas with the whole garlic cloves and bay leaves in water to cover by 5 cm/2 in. in a large pan, partially covered with a lid, adding more water if necessary, for 1–1¼ hours or until tender. Drain the chickpeas and discard the garlic and bay leaves.

Heat the oil in a large, heavy pan over a medium heat. Cook the onion, celery, carrots, chopped garlic, peperoncini and ½ teaspoon of the salt, covered, stirring occasionally, until the vegetables are softened, about 12 minutes. Add the chickpeas, tomatoes, 225 ml/1 cup water and the remaining ½ teaspoon salt and simmer, uncovered, until the vegetables are tender and the sauce is slightly thickened, about 5 minutes. Stir in the parsley and more salt to taste.

Stir together 110 ml/½ cup warm water (40–45°C/105–115°F) and the salt for the orecchiette in a bowl until the salt has dissolved. Add the semolina in a stream, beating with an electric mixer at medium speed, until a stiff dough forms, about 2 minutes. Transfer the dough to a work surface lightly dusted with semolina and knead with lightly dusted hands until smooth and elastic, about 6 minutes. Divide the dough into 5 pieces and let stand under an overturned bowl for 30 minutes.

Line two trays with kitchen towel and dust with some semolina. Keep the remaining dough covered, and roll one piece into a 35-cm/14-in-long rope (about 2 cm/¾ in. thick) on an unfloured surface. Cut the rope into ½-cm/¼-in. pieces. Dust your thumb with some semolina and press down on each piece of dough, pushing away from you and twisting your thumb slightly to form an indented curled shape (like an ear). Transfer to the lined trays. Repeat with the rest of the dough.

Bring a pan of salted water to a rolling boil, add the orecchiette and cook until they are al dente. Drain and toss with the sauce.

Cook's notes: Orecchiette can be made (but not cooked) 3 days ahead. You can substitute 400 g/14 oz. canned chickpeas, drained and rinsed, for cooked dried ones. Dried chickpeas can be cooked 2 days ahead. Cool completely and chill in their cooking liquid, covered.

Radicchio lasagne

I have a tremendous love of radicchio, having watched it being grown by my father. It's great to grow at home, as it is ready to harvest in just six weeks. There are two varieties: round radicchio, which is the most common, and Treviso, which is long and thin. Do try and get Treviso – order it from your greengrocer if needs be – as it is much less bitter and much more flavourful.

4 heads Treviso radicchio or 2 medium round radicchio

4 tablespoons/¼ cup olive oil

1 medium fennel bulb, stalks and outer layer discarded, and quartered

300 g/11 oz. dried lasagne verdi (green pasta sheets)

85 g/6 tablespoons unsalted butter

1 red onion, finely chopped

55 g/½ cup plain/all-purpose flour

1 garlic clove, crushed

500 ml/2 cups milk

150 g/5½ oz. Gorgonzola cheese, cut into cubes

sea salt and freshly ground black pepper

Serves 4

Preheat the oven to 200°C (400°F) Gas 6.

Quarter the radicchio, wash well and pat dry. Place on a baking sheet and drizzle the radicchio with the oil. Bake in the preheated oven (or put under a preheated grill/broiler) for 10 minutes. The radicchio will change colour and become slightly charred. This is correct, as the flavour will be at its best. Set aside.

Meanwhile, steam the fennel pieces over boiling water, about 12 minutes (it should be slightly al dente). Remove and finely chop.

Cook the lasagne in plenty of rolling boiling, salted water until al dente. Drain and set aside.

Heat the butter in a saucepan over a low-to-medium heat, add the onion and cook until it is softened and golden. Add the flour, garlic and steamed fennel and cook for a few minutes to remove the raw taste from the flour. Now add the milk, and season to taste. Remove from the heat and stir vigorously with a wooden spoon.

Put the pan back on the heat and bring to the boil, stirring continuously until thickened. Add the cubed Gorgonzola and stir well. Check the seasoning.

To assemble the dish, place a layer of sauce in an ovenproof dish, followed by a layer of radicchio and a layer of pasta, and continue in this fashion until all the sauce, radicchio and lasagne have been used up. Finish with sauce on top.

Place in the preheated oven and bake for 20 minutes until golden.

Tian of baked courgettes

1.5 kg/3¼ lbs. tender young courgettes/zucchini

sea salt and freshly ground black pepper

225 g/8 oz. short-grain rice

3 tablespoons olive oil

2 large onions, finely chopped

1 garlic clove, finely chopped

3 eggs

225 g/8 oz. young spinach leaves, shredded

a large handful of fresh flat-leaf parsley, finely chopped

a handful of torn fresh basil leaves

100 g/1 cup Parmesan cheese, freshly grated

2 tablespoons French extra virgin olive oil

Serves 8

Some Provençal dishes take their name from the local earthenware casserole, the tian, in which they are cooked. This particular recipe, provided by Martine Bourdon-Williams of Nice, has a pleasant mixture of different textures and flavours. Make a large amount because you will enjoy it and eat more than you think. I always make this dish when I'm entertaining a large group of students.

Trim the courgettes/zucchini but leave them whole and unpeeled. Boil in a saucepan of salted water for 10 minutes, or steam until tender.

Cook the rice in a separate saucepan of boiling, salted water for 10 minutes, then drain.

Heat 2 tablespoons of the oil in a frying pan/skillet. Add the onion and garlic and sauté for 5 minutes until golden.

Preheat the oven to 200°C (400°F) Gas 6. Grease a large ovenproof dish with the remaining oil.

Turn the cooked courgettes/zucchini into a colander and mash with a potato masher, letting the juices drain away.

In a large bowl, lightly beat the eggs and add the spinach, parsley, basil, Parmesan and pepper, then add the mashed courgettes/zucchini, garlic and onion, along with the rice. Mix well together and taste before adding any salt.

Pour the mixture into the prepared dish and bake in the oven for 30 minutes or until firm and browned on top. Drizzle with the extra virgin olive oil and serve.

Panisse with aubergine and pine nut caviar

In the south of France and Italy, this is an extremely popular pancake. I have enjoyed them served with just salt and oil drizzled on top, but this more elaborate version is rather special. This recipe is excellent for special diets.

FOR THE PANCAKES:

250 g/2 cups chickpea/gram flour, sifted

½ teaspoon ground cumin

1 teaspoon sea salt

6 tablespoons olive oil

2–3 tablespoons groundnut/peanut oil

FOR THE CAVIAR:

3 medium-sized aubergines/eggplant

6 tablespoons fruity extra virgin olive oil, with citrus notes

1 red onion, finely chopped

sea salt and freshly ground black pepper

100 g/⅔ cup pine nuts

6 sprigs of fresh mint leaves, plus extra, chopped, to serve

a small handful of fresh flat-leaf parsley

a small handful of fresh coriander/cilantro

juice of 1 lemon

3 tablespoons light tahini paste

1 garlic clove

paprika to taste, and for garnishing

2 small pinches of chilli powder

TO SERVE:

300 g/1¼ cups plain yoghurt

Serves 4–6

To make the pancake batter, place the flour, cumin and salt in a mixing bowl. Make a well in the centre and pour in the olive oil. Gradually whisk in 450 ml/2 cups water to make a smooth batter. Leave to rest in a cool place for at least 2 hours.

For the caviar, heat the oven to 200°C (400°F) Gas 6. Set aside one aubergine/eggplant for later and place the remaining two on a lined baking sheet. Bake for 45 minutes until soft and shrivelled.

Meanwhile, dice the reserved aubergine/eggplant into 1-cm/½-in. pieces. Heat 3 tablespoons of the extra virgin olive oil in a saucepan and add the onion and a pinch of salt. Cook, stirring over a moderate heat, for 10 minutes until the onion is soft but not coloured. Add the diced aubergine/eggplant and continue to cook, stirring, for 15–20 minutes until it is tender. Season with salt and pepper.

Place the pine nuts in a frying pan/skillet and toast for about 3 minutes over a moderate heat, stirring to prevent them from burning. Stir two-thirds of the pine nuts into the onion and aubergine/eggplant mixture and reserve the rest for garnishing.

When the aubergines/eggplant in the oven are cooked, remove and leave to cool. Split in half and scoop out the flesh into a sieve/strainer over a bowl. Press down to remove excess water. Place the aubergine/eggplant flesh in a blender or food processor and add the mint, parsley, coriander/cilantro, lemon juice, tahini paste, garlic clove, paprika and chilli powder. Blend until smooth and add the remaining 3 tablespoons olive oil. Taste and adjust the seasoning. Mix the purée with the onion, aubergine/eggplant and pine nut mixture and keep it warm while you prepare the pancakes.

Heat the groundnut/peanut oil in a frying pan/skillet (18 cm/7 in. in diameter). Pour in a ladleful of batter and cook for about 2 minutes, then carefully flip and cook for a further minute. Slide the pancake onto a baking sheet lined with baking parchment and keep warm. Cook the rest of the batter this way, adding more oil to the pan if necessary.

To serve, place a pancake on a plate and top with the caviar and a little yoghurt. Scatter with chopped mint and the remaining pine nuts.

Fish

Mackerel with apple, watercress and ajo blanco

6 mackerel fillets, skin scored

1 tablespoon olive oil

juice of 1 lemon

3 medium-sized crisp, sweet apples, cored and sliced

150 g/5½ oz. watercress

2 tablespoons red wine vinegar

1 small red onion, finely sliced into half moons for garnish

FOR THE AJO BLANCO:

50 g/1¾ oz. stale white bread, crusts removed (sourdough is best)

125 g/1 cup blanched white almonds

1 garlic clove, chopped

1 tablespoon white balsamic vinegar

2 tablespoons Spanish extra virgin olive oil

sea salt and freshly ground black pepper

Serves 6

This is a fine combination of flavours. I first demonstrated this recipe at a farm called Burwash Manor, near Cambridge, England. It was their annual Apple Day and the response was very encouraging!

Start by making the ajo blanco. Soak the bread in a bowl with cold water for 15 minutes. Meanwhile, finely grind the almonds in a food processor. Pour in 100 ml/scant ½ cup of cold water and combine to blend until you have a loose paste. Add the garlic and blend. Drain the bread and add to the almond paste, along with the vinegar and extra virgin olive oil. Season to taste. Cover and transfer to the fridge for at least 1 hour.

Heat a griddle/grill pan until hot. Season and brush the mackerel with the oil. Cook for 4 minutes, skin-side down. Turn and cook for a further 2 minutes. Squeeze the lemon juice over the fillets. Mix the apples, watercress and red wine vinegar together and divide between plates. Top with the mackerel, ajo blanco and slices of red onion.

Poached turbot with watercress oil

Turbot is a treat and is certainly one to reserve for special occasions. The watercress oil is a perfect companion for this oh-so delicious fish.

6 fillets of turbot, about 190 g/ 6½ oz. each, skinned

FOR THE COURT BOUILLON:

1 carrot

1 stick/rib of celery, sliced

1 small onion, sliced

2 teaspoons salt

1 teaspoon black peppercorns

a handful of fresh flat-leaf parsley

200 ml/¾ cup dry Vermouth

FOR THE WATERCRESS OIL:

2 tablespoons rock salt

150 g/15½ oz. watercress, plus extra to garnish

sea salt and freshly ground black pepper

120 ml/½ cup extra virgin rapeseed/canola oil

3 tablespoons extra virgin olive oil, not peppery or heavy but appley/green

3 teaspoons freshly squeezed lime juice

Serves 6

Place the ingredients for the court bouillon in a saucepan with 1.4 litres/6 cups water and bring to the boil. Turn down the heat and simmer for 30 minutes. Strain the vegetables through a sieve into a roasting tin. Discard the vegetables and set aside.

Have a bowl of iced water ready for the watercress oil. Fill a saucepan with water and add the rock salt. Bring to the boil and add the watercress. Blanch for 25 seconds, then drain and immediately immerse in the bowl of cold water. Drain the watercress and squeeze out as much moisture as possible. Pat dry with paper towels and roughly chop. Place the watercress in a blender or food processor with a little salt and pepper and half of the rapeseed/canola oil, and blend for 20 seconds. With the motor running slowly, add the remaining rapeseed/canola oil, the olive oil and lime juice. Season to taste and set aside.

For the turbot, bring the court bouillon to a gentle simmer in a roasting tin on the hob/stovetop. Carefully place the turbot fillets in the liquid and poach for 8–12 minutes until the fillets turn opaque. The cooking time will depend on the thickness of the fillets. Do not allow the liquid to boil. Lift out the fillets and place them on a warm plate with watercress to garnish and a drizzle of the watercress oil.

Black cod with olives and potatoes in parchment

A favourite Barese recipe (often named after San Nicola, the guardian saint of sailors), these little packets seal in the fish and vegetable juices, with the potato slices insulating the fish from the heat of the oven. The olives and lemon slices emphasize the bright flavours of the dish.

250 g/9 oz. small new potatoes

3 tablespoons plus 1 teaspoon olive oil

1 tablespoon plus 2 teaspoons fresh oregano, finely chopped

2¼ teaspoons fine sea salt

8 x 150-g/5½-oz. pieces skinless black cod, Pacific cod or haddock fillet (about 2.5 cm/1 in. thick), any bones removed

1 lemon, very thinly sliced

6 garlic cloves, thinly sliced

125 g/1 cup Kalamata black olives, pitted and cut into slivers

a handful of fresh flat-leaf parsley

delicate extra virgin olive oil for drizzling

Equipment:

an adjustable blade slicer, 27.5–37.5 cm/11–15 in.

Serves 8

Preheat the oven to 200°C (400°F) Gas 6, with a baking sheet on the bottom shelf/rack.

Cut the potatoes into very thin slices using the slicer. Toss the potatoes with 2 tablespoons of the oil, 1 teaspoon oregano and ¼ teaspoon sea salt. Divide the potatoes among 8 large squares of parchment, arranging them in the centre so that they overlap slightly, then top with a piece of fish.

Sprinkle each fillet with a scant ¼ teaspoon sea salt, then top each with a lemon slice, a few garlic and olive slivers, parsley, ½ teaspoon oregano and ½ teaspoon oil.

Gather the sides of the parchment up and over the fish to form a pouch, leaving no openings, and tie tightly with kitchen string. Put the packages on the hot baking sheet and bake until the fish is just cooked through, 15–22 minutes.

Cut open the parchment parcels to serve and drizzle with the extra virgin olive oil.

Cook's note: The fish can be assembled in parchment 4 hours ahead and kept chilled.

Sicilian-style tuna with fennel and chillies

FOR THE MARINADE:

125 ml/½ cup Sicilian extra virgin olive oil

4 fresh red chillies/chiles, deseeded and finely chopped

4 garlic cloves, crushed

grated zest and freshly squeezed juice of 3 unwaxed lemons

25 g/a large handful of fresh flat-leaf parsley, finely chopped

sea salt and freshly ground black pepper

FOR THE TUNA:

4 x 125-g/4-oz. tuna steaks

2 fennel bulbs, finely sliced through the root

2 red onions, sliced

2–3 tablespoons olive oil

TO SERVE:

crusty bread

Serves 4

My lasting memories of Sicily are travelling on a business trip with my father. Business was conducted not in an office restaurant but in a fish market, then in the car, and then in the kitchen where this dish was prepared for us. I shall never forget this lunch. I experienced such convivial hospitality and memorable food that I have now written about it in two books.

For the marinade, mix all the ingredients together in a bowl and season to taste.

For the tuna, place the steaks in a shallow dish and cover with 2–3 spoonfuls of the marinade. Reserve the remaining marinade.

Place a griddle/grill pan or frying pan/skillet over a medium heat. Toss the fennel and onions with the oil, then cook for 5 minutes on each side to soften. Place on a plate and drizzle with the reserved marinade.

Fry the tuna in the griddle/grill pan or frying pan/skillet until cooked to your liking, approximately 4–5 minutes on each side.

Serve the tuna steaks on the vegetables with some crusty bread to soak up the juices.

Swordfish kebabs with walnut sauce

Any firm fish works well with this extremely tasty mixture. Swordfish and mint are firm favourites as a flavour combination, or swordfish and parsley.

1 kg/2¼ lbs. swordfish, skin removed and cut into 2 cm/¾ in. cubes

grated zest and freshly squeezed juice of 2 unwaxed lemons

175 ml/¾ cup olive oil

a handful of fresh mint, finely chopped

sea salt and freshly ground black pepper

large handful of fresh bay leaves

2 unwaxed lemons, cut into wedges

FOR THE WALNUT SAUCE:

125 g/1¼ cups fresh walnut halves

1 large garlic clove

160 ml/⅔ cup olive or walnut oil

1 slice of white or brown sourdough, soaked in water

juice of 1 lemon

sea salt and freshly ground black pepper

Serves 6

Put the fish cubes, lemon zest and juice, olive oil, mint, salt and pepper in a large bowl. Mix to coat, cover with clingfilm/plastic wrap and leave in the fridge for a minimum of 1 hour.

Remove the fish from the marinade and thread onto skewers, alternating with bay leaves and lemon wedges.

Cook under a medium grill/broiler, turning after 10 minutes and brushing with the marinade. Alternatively, cook on a hot barbecue/gas or charcoal grill for 6 minutes, brushing with the marinade.

Preheat the oven to 200°C (400°F) Gas 6, and line a baking sheet with baking parchment. Toast the walnuts on the lined baking sheet for 8 minutes.

Grind the walnuts in a food processor or using a pestle and mortar with the garlic, oil, bread (squeezed dry) and the freshly squeezed lemon juice. You should have a thick, smooth sauce. Adjust the seasoning to your taste.

FOR THE SALSA VERDE:

4 pickled cucumbers or big gherkins

a large bunch of fresh flat-leaf parsley

a large handful of fresh mint leaves

25 g/3 tablespoons salted capers, rinsed and dried

2 garlic cloves, peeled and chopped

2 large eggs, hard-boiled

4 tablespoons fresh white breadcrumbs

2 tablespoons white wine vinegar

1 tablespoon caster/granulated sugar

8 tablespoons extra virgin olive oil

FOR THE POLPETTONE:

250 g/9 oz. minced/ground beef

250 g/9 oz. minced/ground veal (preferably rose veal)

1 small red onion, very finely chopped

50 g/2 oz. thinly sliced pancetta, very finely chopped

1 garlic clove, crushed

grated zest of 1 unwaxed lemon

90 g/1½ cups fresh white breadcrumbs

3 tablespoons flat-leaf parsley

25 g/1¼ cup freshly grated Parmesan cheese

1 large egg, beaten

FOR THE COURGETTE AND LENTIL SALAD:

3 tablespoons garlic-infused extra virgin olive oil

375 g/scant 2 cups green lentils, rinsed

1 onion, halved

2 bay leaves

1 red (bell) pepper, cut into batons

6 courgettes/zucchini, about 1 kg/2¼ lbs., cut into 5-mm/¼-in thick slices

freshly squeezed juice of 1 unwaxed lemon

2 tablespoons extra virgin olive oil

2 tablespoons chopped fresh flat-leaf parsley

sea salt and freshly ground black pepper

Serves 4–6

Meat and poultry

Polpettone with courgette and lentil salad

Both the polpettone (or, to give it its more prosaic English name, meatloaf) and the salad can be made in advance. The polpettone can be heated through or served cold and any leftovers make a delicious ciabatta filling. If you cannot find veal, use double the quantity of minced/ground beef.

For the salsa verde, finely chop the cucumbers or gherkins, parsley, mint, capers and garlic. Peel and mash the hard-boiled eggs. Put all the ingredients in a blender or food processor and blend everything together to produce a smooth, green sauce.

Preheat the oven to 200°C (400°C) Gas 6. Base-line a 1.5-litre/1½-quart loaf pan with baking parchment. Place the beef and veal in a mixing bowl and add the onion, pancetta, garlic, lemon zest, two-thirds of the breadcrumbs, parsley, Parmesan and egg. Season with a ¼ teaspoon salt and some pepper.

Tip the mixture into the loaf pan and smooth out to the edges. Sprinkle the top with the remaining breadcrumbs. Cook in the oven for 30 minutes until a skewer inserted into the centre of the meat feels piping hot to the touch. Take care not to burn your fingers! Leave to cool in the pan for at least 15 minutes, then lift out onto a plate.

For the salad, cook the lentils with 250 ml/1 cup water in a medium-sized pan with the onion and bay leaves. Add the (bell) pepper and courgettes/zucchini halfway through cooking. After 15 minutes, when the lentils are tender, add the lemon juice, oil and parsley, and season to taste. Serve with the meatloaf and salsa verde.

Salmoriglio lamb with borlotti and green bean salad

Salmoriglio is a Sicilian sauce of oregano and olive oil used for marinating fish and meat, or to dress salad. Here it is used to marinate lamb and doubles up as a salad dressing.

5 garlic cloves, 4 crushed

1 tablespoon chilli/hot red pepper flakes

3 tablespoons light brown sugar

thickly grated zest and freshly squeezed juice of 2 unwaxed lemons

a small handful of oregano leaves, chopped

100 ml/6 tablespoons extra virgin olive oil

2-kg/4½-lbs. butterflied leg of lamb

sea salt and freshly ground black pepper

FOR THE SALAD:

3 red onions, thickly sliced

light brown sugar, to taste

3 tablespoons balsamic vinegar

2 x 400-g/14-oz. cans borlotti beans, drained and rinsed

300 g/11 oz. small vine-ripened tomatoes, halved

100 g/3½ oz. green beans, blanched

15 black olives, stoned/pitted

Serves 6

Make the marinade by mixing the 4 crushed garlic cloves, the chilli/hot red pepper flakes, brown sugar, lemon zest, three-quarters of the lemon juice, half the oregano and 2 tablespoons of the olive oil in a small bowl. Season the meat all over and lay it in a glass ovenproof dish. Pour over the marinade and massage it into the lamb. Cover with clingfilm/plastic wrap and refrigerate overnight or for at least 2 hours. Bring back to room temperature before cooking.

Preheat the oven to 180°C (350°F) Gas 4. Arrange the onion slices in a large roasting pan. Season well and drizzle with some of the remaining olive oil, a little sugar and the balsamic vinegar. Roast for 30 minutes and then remove from the oven. Put the borlotti beans in a dish and top with the tomatoes, green beans, olives and onions.

Chop the remaining oregano and garlic clove until very fine. Put in a bowl with some seasoning and the lemon juice.

Heat a barbecue/gas or charcoal grill. Cook the lamb for 15 minutes on each side on indirect heat for pink meat. Leave to rest for 10 minutes. If cooking indoors, chargrill or sear the lamb in a hot griddle/grill pan or frying pan/skillet until browned on both sides, then finish in a preheated 200°C (400°F) Gas 6 oven for 25–30 minutes. Serve the meat sliced with the salad and a bowl of the oregano sauce.

Rack of lamb with beetroot and walnut salsa

Get your butcher to French trim the racks so that they look neat and are easy to eat. Some supermarkets sell prepared French-trimmed racks of lamb.

10 beetroots/beets, about
1 kg/2¼ lbs., scrubbed clean

7 tablespoons extra virgin olive oil

4 garlic cloves, left whole

sea salt and freshly ground
black pepper

40 g/⅓ cup fresh walnut halves

1 tablespoon Dijon mustard

1½ tablespoons balsamic vinegar

1 tablespoon freshly squeezed
lemon juice

2 tablespoons fresh mint leaves,
finely chopped

50 g/2 large handfuls of
rocket/arugula

3–4 racks of lamb, about 1 kg/
2¼ lbs. total weight

Serves 6

Preheat the oven to 200°C (400°F) Gas 6. Place the beetroots/beets in a roasting pan and pour over 3 tablespoons of the olive oil. Mix well, add the garlic cloves and season with salt and pepper. Cover with aluminium foil and roast in the oven for 1¼–1½ hours or until the beetroots/beets are cooked through but still firm.

Meanwhile, heat a small frying pan/skillet and add the walnut halves. Dry-fry over a moderate heat for 2–3 minutes, stirring, until the walnuts are lightly toasted. Remove from the heat, cool, then roughly chop. Set aside.

Remove the beetroots/beets from the oven, leave until cool enough to handle, then peel off their skins and halve them. Return to the oven for 25 minutes. Discard the garlic cloves, leave the beetroots/beets to cool, then finely dice the flesh and place it in a mixing bowl. Mix in the remaining 4 tablespoons olive oil, the mustard, balsamic vinegar, lemon juice, chopped walnuts and mint. Season with salt and pepper. Roughly chop the rocket/arugula and stir it into the beetroot/beets mixture.

Place the racks of lamb in a large roasting pan and season well. Roast the lamb for 20–30 minutes, depending on how pink you like your lamb, then remove from the oven, cover and leave to rest for 10 minutes. Either slice the racks into individual chops, giving three per person, or halve each rack. Serve with the salsa on the side.

Pork roast braised with milk and fresh herbs

Simmering a pork roast with milk and a generous handful of herbs results in very tender meat with rich silky juices. Many Italians will leave the milk curds that form alongside the meat where they are, but I strain them out for a more refined sauce.

50 ml/3 tablespoons olive oil

2–2.25-kg/4½–5-lb. boneless pork shoulder roast (without skin), tied

3 juniper berries, crushed (see Cook's notes)

2 large sprigs of fresh rosemary

2 large sprigs of fresh sage

1 sprig of fresh or 4 dried bay leaves

1 garlic clove

fine sea salt and freshly ground black pepper

50 ml/3 tablespoons white wine vinegar

1 litre/1 quart whole milk

Serves 6–8

Preheat the oven to 180°C (350°F) Gas 4 with the shelf/rack in the middle of the oven.

Heat the oil in a large, wide ovenproof heavy saucepan over a medium heat, then lightly brown the pork on all sides with the juniper berries and herbs for 8–10 minutes in total.

Add the garlic clove and sprinkle the pork with 1 teaspoon fine sea salt and ½ teaspoon black pepper. Cook until the garlic is golden, about 1 minute. Pour the white wine vinegar over the roast and briskly simmer until it is reduced by half.

Pour the milk over the roast and bring to a bare simmer. Cover the saucepan and braise the pork in the oven, turning it occasionally, for 2–2½ hours until tender (the milk will form curds).

Transfer the roast to a carving board and loosely cover. Strain the juices through a fine-mesh sieve/strainer into a bowl (discard the solids) and skim off the fat. Return the juices to the saucepan and boil until flavourful and reduced to about 450 ml/2 cups. Season to taste with salt and pepper.

Slice the pork and serve it moistened with the juices.

Cook's notes: Juniper berries can be found in the spice aisle at supermarkets. The pork can be braised a day ahead and chilled in the liquid, uncovered, until cool, then covered. Bring to room temperature, then reheat and proceed with the recipe.

Sweet and sour spare ribs

This recipe has special memories for me. My mummy made this when we were teenagers for family parties and gatherings. We were always eating Italian food, and when she produced this dish, we thought we were so exotic!

2 kg/4½ lbs. pork spare ribs

sea salt

2 tablespoons groundnut/peanut oil

FOR THE SAUCE:

2 tablespoons groundnut/peanut oil

1 large onion, finely chopped

1 large garlic clove, crushed

1 tablespoon cider vinegar

1 tablespoon tomato purée/paste

1 tablespoon tamari soy sauce

4 teaspoons soft light brown sugar

1 tablespoon clear honey

300ml/1¼ cups chicken stock
(fresh is best)

juice of 1 freshly squeezed lemon

freshly ground black pepper

Serves 6–8

Preheat the oven to 190°C (375°F) Gas 5. Sprinkle the pork with salt to taste and place in a roasting tin. Pour over the oil and roast for 25 minutes.

Remove the pork from the oven and use a sharp knife to cut it into individual ribs.

To prepare the sauce, heat 1 tablespoon of the oil in a small pan, add the onion and cook gently until coloured. Add the garlic and cook gently. Add all the remaining sauce ingredients, along with pepper to taste. Mix well.

Return the meat to the roasting pan, pour over the sauce and continue to roast, covered with foil, for 1–1½ hours. Serve with rice or your favourite accompaniment.

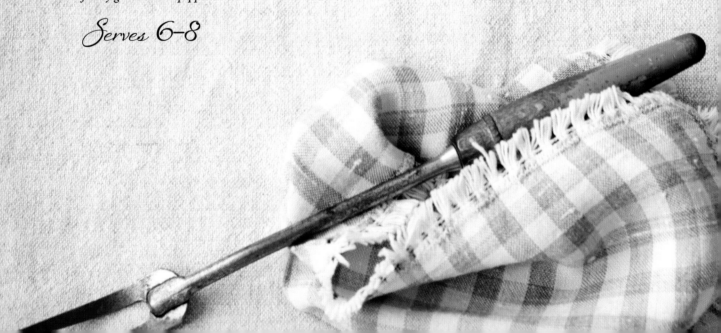

Sweet, sticky Chinese chicken

4 Maryland pieces of chicken
(leg and thigh together)

FOR THE MARINADE:

grated zest and juice of 1 organic
(unwaxed) orange

3 tablespoons clear honey

2 tablespoons muscovado/
light brown sugar

1 tablespoon Chinese five-spice
powder

2 tablespoons soy sauce

2 tablespoons toasted sesame oil

TO SERVE:

crisp salad

Serves 8

As an Italian, I love Italian food. However, as
I live with a gourmet husband whose palate
extends across the globe, I sometimes have to
step outside Italy. This easy, home-from-work
recipe fits the bill.

Put the chicken in a sealable plastic bag. Mix all the marinade
ingredients together and pour over the chicken. Seal the bag
and squidge it together to coat the chicken well. Refrigerate
for at least 2 hours (overnight is better).

Preheat the oven to 180°C (350°F) Gas 4. Tip the chicken
and marinade into a large roasting tin and spread it out evenly.
Roast for 45 minutes until the chicken is cooked through with
no pink meat, and the juices run clear.

Remove the cooked chicken from the oven and, if liked, finish
in a hot griddle/grill pan, browning the pieces skin-side down
for about 5 minutes until the chicken is crisp and slightly
charred. Serve with a crisp salad.

Nonna Ferrigno's chicken casserole

sea salt and freshly ground black pepper

2 tablespoons Italian '00' flour

8 chicken thighs, bone and skin on or off, depending on your preference

3 tablespoons olive oil

2 celery stalks/ribs, finely chopped

1 medium carrot, diced

1 red onion, diced

150 g/5½ oz. chestnut/cremini mushrooms, coarsely chopped

1 garlic clove, crushed

3 tablespoons white wine vinegar

2 sprigs of fresh rosemary, leaves finely chopped

1 teaspoon dried mixed herbs

3 bay leaves

6 tablespoons Italian passata/strained tomatoes

6 medium potatoes, peeled and quartered (not too small)

a handful of fresh flat-leaf parsley, chopped

TO SERVE:

focaccia or crusty bread

Serves 8

This recipe is revisited so frequently in my home, not just for its taste, but also for its ease of cooking. It is tasty, satisfying and also a one-pot meal, which is very useful for time-short mums. I have experimented over the years with various combinations, sometimes using smoky bacon, lardons or pancetta. All of these are good variations, but are not necessary.

Add a little salt and pepper to the flour, and coat the chicken in it.

Heat a flameproof casserole dish, add the olive oil and heat gently. Add the chicken, cook until coloured and then remove. Add more oil if necessary and add the celery, carrot, onion, mushrooms and garlic. Cook for 5 minutes until lightly golden. Add the chicken, vinegar, 500 ml/2 cups water, herbs, passata/strained tomatoes and potatoes. Season with salt and pepper.

Simmer for 45 minutes, checking that the casserole is not drying up and stirring it periodically.

Garnish with the parsley and serve with focaccia or crusty bread to mop up the juices.

Marinated duck breasts with cucumber and mint salad

This recipe is a little bit more demanding in terms of ingredients and effort, but it is well worth it! The combination of Asian flavours is very authentic, making the dish a perennial hit with the family and dinner guests alike.

FOR THE MARINADE:

1 cinnamon stick

1 star anise

2 teaspoons coriander seeds

3 cm/1¼ in. fresh ginger, peeled and grated

2 medium shallots, finely diced

1 tablespoon sea salt

3 tablespoons rice vinegar

2 duck breasts

FOR THE SALAD:

125 g/4½ oz. cucumber, sliced in matchsticks

1 teaspoon sea salt

1 red onion, finely chopped

2 tablespoons white wine vinegar

1 tablespoon rapeseed/canola oil

2 tablespoons fruity extra virgin olive oil

1 tablespoon caster/granulated sugar

a large handful of fresh mint leaves, stalks removed and chopped

a bag of pea shoots, approximately 110 g/4 oz.

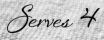

Serves 4

To make the marinade, dry roast the spices in a frying pan/skillet for 1½–2 minutes until fragrant, then pound in a pestle and mortar with the ginger and shallots. Mix in the salt and rice vinegar, then rub over the duck breasts in a glass dish. Cover with clingfilm/plastic wrap and refrigerate for a minimum of 2 hours or overnight.

For the salad, toss the cucumber with 1 teaspoon salt in a colander. Drain in the sink for 20 minutes. Scatter the cucumber slices on paper towels and pat dry. Soak the red onion in cold water for 10 minutes, then drain.

Mix the cucumber, red onion, vinegar, oils, sugar and mint together in a bowl. Season with salt and pepper, and set aside.

Preheat the oven to 180°C (350°F) Gas 4. Brush the marinade off the duck breasts and place skin-side down in a cold, ovenproof frying pan/skillet. Cook over a medium heat for 15 minutes, and pour away any excess fat.

Turn the breasts over and cook for 2 minutes, then place in the oven for 10 minutes.

Slice the duck and serve with the cucumber salad, with the pea shoots mixed in.

Accompaniments, sauces and spreads

Roasted Jersey Royals wrapped in pancetta with thyme dressing

500 g/1 lb. 2 oz. Jersey Royals or other new white potatoes, lightly washed

sea salt and freshly ground black pepper

15–20 slices of pancetta, cut into strips

1 teaspoon fresh thyme leaves

1 tablespoon olive oil

50 ml/3 tablespoons crème fraîche or sour cream

½ tablespoon white wine vinegar

½ teaspoon crushed dried peperoncini chillies/chiles

1 tablespoon extra virgin olive oil

chopped fresh chervil, to garnish

Serves 4–6

Roasting this most delicate potato is a little unconventional, but it intensifies the buttery consistency. You can also use Nicola, Elvira or Charlotte potatoes.

Preheat the oven to 180°C (350°F) Gas 4.

Put the potatoes in a pan and cover with cold salted water. Bring to the boil and cook for 5 minutes, then refresh them under cold water until they have cooled down. They should be al dente. Drain and set aside.

Lay out a pancetta strip for each potato. Season with salt and pepper and half of the thyme. Roll each potato in a pancetta strip and place on a baking sheet lined with baking parchment. Drizzle over the olive oil.

Roast for 15 minutes, turning halfway during cooking. The pancetta should be crisp and golden.

For the dressing, whisk the crème fraîche or sour cream with the vinegar, peperoncini chillies/chiles, extra virgin olive oil and remaining thyme until smooth. Season, then drizzle the dressing over the potatoes and scatter with chervil.

Swede chips

500 g/1 lb. 2 oz. swede/rutabaga

4 sprigs of fresh rosemary, chopped

2 sprigs of fresh sage, chopped

4 tablespoons/¼ cup olive oil

sea salt

Serves 4–6

Swede/rutabaga is not a glamorous vegetable, but it can be transformed with this very simple treatment. Try it with celeriac/celery root, too.

Preheat the oven to 200°C (400°F) Gas 6. Line a baking sheet with baking parchment.

Peel and cut the swede/rutabaga into 5-cm/2-in. strips. Mix with the herbs and oil, and place on the lined baking sheet.

Roast for 12 minutes. Sprinkle with sea salt to taste and serve.

5 tablespoons rapeseed/canola oil

4 medium leeks, washed well and finely chopped

sea salt

400 g/2 cups cooked chickpeas (⅓ crushed to absorb more flavour)

a handful of fresh flat-leaf parsley, finely chopped

3 tablespoons freshly ground black pepper

1 tablespoon Dijon mustard

1 teaspoon wholegrain mustard

1 tablespoon white wine vinegar

Serves 4-6

Leek and chickpeas with mustard dressing

This is a relaxed dish to serve with meat or fish, or as an appetizer with sourdough on the side. It improves in flavour over time, so it's a good idea to make it in advance.

Heat 2 tablespoons of the oil in a frying pan/skillet, add the leeks and salt to taste and cook until softened. Add the chickpeas, mix well and heat well together. Take off the heat and add the parsley and black pepper.

Mix the mustards, vinegar and remaining oil together, then stir into the leeks and chickpeas and serve.

Italian-style green vegetables

200 g/7 oz. trimmed green beans

200 g/7 oz. tenderstem broccoli

100 g/3½ oz. young spinach leaves

grated zest and freshly squeezed juice of 1 unwaxed lemon

1 mild fresh red chilli/chile, deseeded and finely chopped or a pinch of crushed dried peperoncini chillies/chiles

100 ml/6 tablespoons fruity extra virgin olive oil – Sicilian if possible

sea salt and freshly ground black pepper

Serves 4-6

This very simple treatment of green vegetables is enduringly delicious, and I am thrilled to say so well received whenever I introduce it. Antonia, my little girl, will not eat vegetables done any other way with quite the same relish.

Bring a large pan of water to the boil. Plunge all the vegetables in it for 3 minutes. Drain immediately and place in a bowl.

Add the lemon zest and juice and combine with the extra virgin olive oil. Add the chilli/chile and season the dressing to taste.

Stir the dressing through the vegetables to coat.

FOR THE SEVEN VEGETABLE SAUCE:

125 g/heaping cup dried chickpeas, soaked overnight

2 large onions, finely chopped

2 garlic cloves, finely chopped

½ teaspoon saffron threads

2 teaspoon ground cinnamon

1 teaspoon paprika

a large pinch of cayenne pepper

½ teaspoon ground ginger

1 tablespoon ras el hanout spice mix

sea salt

225 g/8 oz. carrots, cut in half lengthways

½ medium white cabbage, cut into 8 pieces

6 artichoke hearts

1 medium aubergine/eggplant, quartered

225 g/8 oz. small potatoes, peeled and halved

225 g/8 oz. turnips, peeled and sliced

225 g/8 oz. podded broad/fava beans, skinned

125 g/1 scant cup raisins

225 g/8 oz. fresh pumpkin, cut into 5-cm/2-in. slices

2 tomatoes

a bunch of fresh flat-leaf parsley, chopped

a large bunch of fresh coriander/cilantro, chopped

1 tablespoon olive oil

FOR THE COUSCOUS:

450 g/2⅔ cups quick-cook couscous

a pinch of sea salt

4 tablespoons French extra virgin olive oil

1–2 tablespoons unsalted butter

Serves 5–6

Couscous with seven vegetable sauce

Couscous is the national dish of Morocco. In Morocco it is more delicate and less hot and spicy than the Tunisian and Algerian versions now found in France. Seven, considered a lucky number, is the traditional number of vegetables used in the recipe, the choice depending on those in season. This is a one-pot meal, easy to make for large numbers.

To prepare the sauce, drain the chickpeas and put them in a large saucepan. Add 3 litres/3 quarts water, bring to the boil and remove the froth. Add the onions and garlic to the pan with the spices and ras el hanout spice mix. Simmer for at least 30 minutes.

Season with salt when the chickpeas begin to soften.

Add the carrots, cabbage, artichoke hearts, aubergine/eggplant and potatoes, and more water, if necessary and cook for 20 minutes. Add the turnips, broad/ fava beans and raisins and cook for 10 minutes. Next, add the pumpkin and tomatoes and cook for 5 minutes. Add the herbs and oil and cook for a further 5 minutes.

While the vegetables are cooking, prepare the couscous. Put the couscous in a large bowl and pour in 300 ml/1¼ cups water with the salt. Stir well until evenly absorbed. Leave for 10 minutes.

Add a further 300 ml/1¼ cups of water along with the oil and butter. Rub the grains between your palms and make sure that they are all separate. Leave for a further 10 minutes until the grains are swollen and tender but separate.

Steam the couscous, uncovered, in the top half of a steamer over boiling water for about 8 minutes. (When the steam begins to come through the grain, it is ready to serve.)

Turn the couscous onto a large warmed serving dish and crush with a fork to separate the grains. Put the vegetables in the centre and serve immediately.

2 medium garlic cloves

1 teaspoon cumin seeds

1 teaspoon paprika (not too sweet)

2 teaspoons dried thyme or
1 teaspoon fresh thyme

1 mild fresh red chilli/chile, deseeded
and finely chopped or a pinch of crushed
dried peperoncini chillies/chiles

100 ml/6 tablespoons fruity extra virgin
olive oil – Sicilian if possible

sea salt and freshly ground black pepper

*Makes 1 x
75-g/2-½ oz. jar*

Saba de mojo

This is a unique sauce that I have enjoyed on many family holidays to the Canary Islands in search of the sun in March. I was surprised by the number of variations, but think that I have come across a combination of flavours that is very agreeable. Serve with potatoes baked in their skins. This is equally good on toast or with a simple piece of fish.

Crush the garlic and cumin seeds in a pestle and mortar. Add the paprika, thyme, chilli/chile and oil. Season to taste.

Homemade chocolate spread

100 g/3½ oz. dark/bittersweet chocolate (minimum 70% cocoa solids)

100 ml/½ cup whole milk

75 g/1 cup ground hazelnuts, toasted

2 drops vanilla extract

125 ml/½ cup hazelnut oil

3 tablespoons double/heavy cream

Makes
1 x 500-g/1-lb. 2-oz. jar

When I was in Paris last summer, I had a focaccia coated in chocolate and hazelnut spread in a small artisan pizzeria near the Bastille market – it was utterly delicious. This set my imagination racing, and I decided to try making my own. I hope you enjoy it!

Melt the chocolate with the milk in a medium-sized saucepan, and add the hazelnuts and vanilla extract, then the oil, little by little. When cool, add the cream.

Please enjoy in as many ways as possible. It goes very well with focaccia, pancakes, muffins and crackers.

Bread and crackers

Potato and gorgonzola focaccia

FOR THE DOUGH:

2 medium potatoes, peeled and chopped

500–550g/4–4⅓ cups white strong/bread flour, plus extra for sprinkling and kneading

2 teaspoons fine sea salt

15 g/½ oz. fresh yeast, crumbled or 7 g/¼ oz. dried/active dry yeast

250 ml/1 cup water at body temperature

3 tablespoons olive oil

FOR THE TOPPING:

1 x 400-g/14-oz. can Italian plum tomatoes, drained and chopped

1 tablespoon fresh oregano, chopped

2 tablespoons fresh basil, torn

1 garlic clove, finely chopped

½ teaspoon freshly ground black pepper

375 g/13 oz. quartered artichoke hearts in marinated olive oil

250 g/9 oz. Gorgonzola cheese, crumbled

150 g/5½ oz. mozzarella, shredded

TO SERVE:

fruity extra virgin olive oil

Makes 1

Potato in dough is quite remarkable. This is a firm family favourite for sharing at gatherings or picnics.

In a covered saucepan, boil the potatoes for 10–15 minutes or until they are tender. Drain and mash them, then leave to cool slightly.

In a large bowl, mix two thirds of the flour with the salt. Dissolve the yeast in 2 tablespoons of the water and add it to a well in the centre of the flour with the olive oil. Mix for a few minutes, then stir in the potatoes and as much of the remaining flour as you can.

On a lightly floured work surface, knead in enough of the remaining flour to make a stiff dough that is both smooth and elastic. This will take about 8–10 minutes. Shape the dough into a ball and place it in an oiled bowl, turning it once to grease the surface. Cover it with a damp, clean dish towel and leave it to rise in a warm place until it has doubled in size, approximately 1 hour.

Knock back the dough, cover and let it rest for 10 minutes.

Grease a 38 x 25 x 2.5 cm/15 x 10 x 1 in. baking tray. Press the dough into the tray. If it is sticky, sprinkle the surface with 1 tablespoon of extra flour. Using your fingertips, make small indentations in the dough. Cover and leave it to prove until it has nearly doubled in size, about 30 minutes.

Meanwhile, preheat the oven to 190°C (375°F) Gas 5.

For the topping, mix the tomatoes, oregano, basil, garlic and pepper and spoon evenly over the dough. Place the artichoke hearts over the tomato sauce mixture. Cover with the Gorgonzola and shredded mozzarella. Bake for 35 minutes. Serve hot, drizzled with the extra virgin olive oil.

Sardinian pizza

I have always dreamed of opening a pizzeria, and I think that this particular recipe would be my signature pizza.

FOR THE PIZZA DOUGH:

*15 g/½ oz. fresh yeast or
7 g/¼ oz. dried/active dry yeast*

4 tablespoons water at body temperature

225 g/1¾ cups white strong/bread flour, plus extra for sprinkling

1 teaspoon salt

65 g/2¼ oz. unsalted butter

1 large egg, beaten

olive oil

FOR THE TOPPING:

5 tablespoons olive oil

750 g/1 lb. 10 oz. onions, finely sliced

500g/1 lb. 2 oz. ripe tomatoes, skinned and roughly chopped

sea salt and freshly ground black pepper

55 g/2 oz. anchovy fillets

a few black olives, halved and stoned/pitted

a handful of fresh oregano

TO SERVE:
chilli oil

Serves 8

To make the dough, blend the yeast with the water. Mix the flour and salt together in a large bowl, rub in the butter and make a well in the centre. Put in the egg and the yeast mixture and combine to a firm but pliable dough, adding more water if necessary. When the dough has come away cleanly from the sides of the bowl, turn out onto a floured work surface and knead thoroughly for 10 minutes. Gather into a ball, place into a clean oiled bowl and cover and leave to rise until doubled in size, about 1½ hours.

When the dough has risen, turn it out onto a floured work surface, divide into two and knead each piece lightly. Place in two well-oiled 20–23 cm/8–9 in. pans and press out with floured knuckles. Cover the pans and preheat the oven to 200°C (400°F) Gas 6, while you prepare the topping.

To make the topping, heat 5 tablespoons of the olive oil in a heavy-bottomed frying pan/skillet and sauté the onion gently, covered, stirring now and then, until soft, about 20 minutes. Add the tomatoes and seasoning and cook, uncovered, until the sauce is thick. Leave to cool.

When cold, divide the topping between the pizzas, spreading it evenly. Criss-cross the surface with strips of anchovy and put the olive halves in the spaces. Sprinkle with oregano and bake in the preheated oven for 25 minutes, until golden brown and bubbling. Serve with chilli oil.

Herb spelt bread

This bread has become a real passion of mine and I serve it to guests whenever I possibly can. If I was a betting woman, I would put money on this flour becoming more and more important in the future. It does contain gluten, but it is wheat-free, and as a teacher, I am finding that more and more of my students suffer from food intolerances. As this bread is a one-rise bread, it is easy to fit around our hectic lifestyles. Because of the short protein strands of the grain, a short knead and one rise is all that is necessary. Please feel free to experiment with white and wholegrain. I love the nutty texture of this bread and I sometimes even make grissini with this dough.

500 g/4 cups wholegrain spelt flour, plus extra for sprinkling and kneading

2 teaspoons sea salt

3 teaspoons fresh rosemary, coarsely chopped

2 teaspoons freshly ground black pepper

2 tablespoons rapeseed/canola oil

1 tablespoon fragrant honey such as acacia or rosemary honey

7 g/¼ oz. fresh yeast or 1 teaspoon dried/active dry yeast

400 ml/1¾ cups water at body temperature (you will need to adjust the quantity if using white spelt)

Makes 2

In a large bowl, add the flour, salt, rosemary and black pepper and mix well. Make a reservoir in the middle of the flour, add the oil and honey and then the yeast and water.

Mix well and turn out of the bowl onto a lightly floured work surface. Knead, adding more flour as necessary. The dough should be strong, soft and silky. Knead for approximately 8 minutes.

Shape into two baguettes and place on a baking tray lined with parchment, side by side. Cover and leave for 40 minutes.

Preheat the oven to 180°C (360°F) Gas 5. Bake the loaves until they are golden brown and sound hollow when you tap the underside. Cool on a wire rack.

Enjoy with oil or butter.

Taralli

These crunchy little olive oil and black pepper biscuits hail from Puglia and are very addictive. We serve these in Italy with aperitivos, but they are also excellent picnic snacks. In Puglia these biscuits are available everywhere, but homemade ones are unparalleled. Try adding fennel seeds as they work very well too.

150 g / 1 cup plus 3 tablespoons Italian '00' flour, plus extra for sprinkling and kneading

40 g / ⅓ cup semolina (fine)

1 teaspoon freshly ground black pepper or 2 teaspoons lightly crushed fennel seeds, if using

2 teaspoons sea salt

70 ml / ⅓ cup dry white wine

70 ml / ⅓ cup extra virgin olive oil, from Puglia if possible

Makes 30

Mix together the flour, semolina, pepper or fennel seeds, half the salt, wine and oil. Knead on a floured surface until smooth and elastic, about 2 minutes. Place the dough in a lightly oiled bowl, cover and leave to relax for approximately 45 minutes to 1 hour.

Bring 900 ml / scant 4 cups water to the boil and add the remaining salt.

Halve the dough and cut each half into 10 pieces. Keep the remaining dough covered. Roll one piece of dough into a 50 cm / 10-in. long rope. Cut the rope into 5 pieces, then roll each piece into 10 cm / 4 in. ropes. Connect the ends to form an overlapping ring. Continue with the remaining dough, keeping the taralli covered.

Preheat the oven to 180°C (350°F) Gas 5. Oil two baking trays.

Boil the rings in batches until they float, approximately 3 minutes. Transfer with a slotted spoon to the oiled baking trays and bake until golden and crisp, approximately 30 minutes. Cool on wire racks and enjoy.

Lemon, lime and cardamom crisp crackers

I'm a passionate breadmaker and these wonderfully crispy crackers are the result of a happy experiment. The lemon and lime zest are a perfect partner to the cardamom. I like to serve these crackers with ice cream or soft fruit as the crunch of the crackers counterbalances their velvety texture. A sprinkle of icing/confectioners' sugar gives them a lovely finish.

15 g/½ oz. fresh yeast or
7 g/¼ oz. dried/active dry yeast

250 g/9 oz. strong white unbleached flour, plus extra for sprinkling

½ teaspoon sea salt

50 ml/3 tablespoons olive/coconut oil, plus extra to stretch and roll the dough

zest of 1 unwaxed lemon

zest of 1 lime

2 teaspoons finely ground cardamom or 8 pods finely ground in a pestle and mortar

125 g/⅔ cup granulated sugar

TO SERVE:

vanilla icing/confectioners' sugar

Makes 12–16

Measure 50 ml/3 tablespoons warm water in a jug/measuring cup. Blend the fresh or dried/active dry yeast with a little of this water.

Sift the flour and salt together into a large bowl. Make a well in the centre and add the olive/coconut oil, along with half the lemon, lime, cardamom and sugar mix, the yeast liquid and some of the water. Mix together with a wooden spoon, gradually adding the remaining water, to form a soft dough.

Turn the dough out onto a lightly floured work surface and knead vigorously for 10 minutes until it is soft and satin-like (don't be afraid to add more flour). Place in a lightly oiled large bowl, then turn the dough around to coat with the oil. Cover the bowl with a clean dish towel and leave in a warm place for 1½ hours, or until the dough has doubled in size.

Preheat the oven to 200°C (400°F) Gas 6. Place two oiled baking trays in the bottom of the oven.

Knock down the dough with your knuckles, then turn onto a lightly floured work surface and knead for 2–3 minutes to knock out the air bubbles. Divide the dough in half.

On a lightly floured work surface, preferably marble, roll out the pieces of dough very, very thinly, until 25–30 cm/10–12 in. in diameter. Now lift each cracker onto a cold baking tray and top with the remaining half of the lemon, lime, cardamom and sugar mix.

Carefully slide the prepared crackers off the cold trays directly onto the hot baking trays and immediately bake in the oven for 12 minutes until golden and crisp. Dust with the vanilla icing/confectioners' sugar. When cold, crack them and enjoy!

Desserts

200 g/1⅔ cups Italian '00' flour

½ teaspoon sea salt

1½ teaspoons baking powder

¼ teaspoon bicarbonate of/baking soda

½ teaspoon ground cinnamon

¼ teaspoon ground cloves

¼ teaspoon freshly grated nutmeg

250 ml/1 cup sunflower, olive, groundnut/peanut or grapeseed oil

250 g/1¼ cups packed brown sugar

3 UK large/US extra large eggs, lightly beaten

zest of 1 organic (unwaxed) orange

2 teaspoons vanilla extract

80 g/⅔ cup chopped fresh walnuts, lightly toasted

3 medium carrots, coarsely grated

30 g/⅓ cup desiccated coconut

FOR THE FROSTING:

200 g/1 scant cup cream cheese

95 g/7 tablespoons unsalted butter, softened

1½ tablespoons maple syrup

grated zest of 1 organic (unwaxed) orange

50 g/⅓ cup icing/confectioners' sugar

fresh walnut halves, to decorate

Serves 6–8

My traditional carrot cake

This recipe might in fact be older than me! When I ran my own restaurant, As You Like It, this cake was made for us by a lifelong vegetarian lady who was rather severe in appearance, but gentle and shy. This was her Canadian cousin's recipe. Her cakes were demolished by our customers, one man doing a round trip of 65 kilometres (40 miles) just for a slice! I have changed very little about the recipe.

Preheat the oven to 170°C (325°F) Gas 3. Grease and line the base of a 24-cm/9½-in. loose-based cake pan.

Sift the flour, salt, baking powder, bicarbonate of/baking soda and spices together.

Mix the oil, sugar and eggs together.

Combine the flour mix with the orange zest, vanilla, walnuts, carrots and coconut. Add to the oil and egg mix and combine well. Pour into a greased, round cake pan and bake for 1 hour until a skewer inserted into the cake comes out clean. Leave to cool in the pan for 5 minutes and then turn out.

For the frosting, beat the cream cheese with the softened butter, maple syrup, orange zest and icing/confectioners' sugar. Spread on top of the cake, and decorate with a few walnut halves.

Italian almond apple cake

Born out of a glut of apples, this is the happy result of an experiment.

200 ml/¾ cup olive oil

225 g/1 cup plus 2 tablespoons
light brown sugar

3 UK large/US extra large eggs

225 g/1¾ cups Italian '00' flour

1 teaspoon ground cinnamon

2½ teaspoons baking powder

½ teaspoon cream of tartar

600 g/1¼ lbs. tart dessert apples,
peeled, cored and diced

100 g/⅔ cup raisins

75 g/¾ cup flaked/slivered almonds

grated zest of 2 unwaxed lemons

Serves 6–8

Heat the oven to 180°C (350°F) Gas 4. Line a 20-cm/8-in. springform cake pan with baking parchment. Pour the olive oil into a bowl, add the sugar and beat until smooth with a hand-held electric mixer.

Add the eggs, one at a time, and beat until the mixture has increased in volume and is like thin mayonnaise.

Sift together the flour, cinnamon, baking powder and cream of tartar. Add these dry ingredients gradually to the oil mixture, folding them in with a metal spoon. Now add the apples, raisins, flaked/slivered almonds and lemon zest. Spoon the batter into the cake pan and bake for 1 hour until a skewer inserted in the cake comes out clean. Remove from the pan and leave to cool on a wire rack before serving.

The ultimate banana bread

Oil creates a winning texture in cakes – I hope the following recipe
will convince you! I have had a lifetime's passion for bananas and
a corresponding lifelong pursuit of the best banana recipes.

100 g/⅔ cup dried dates

240 g/2 cups Italian '00' flour

50 g/½ cup porridge/old-fashioned
rolled oats

3 teaspoons baking powder

50 g/½ cup chopped pecans

1 teaspoon salt

60 g/⅓ cup brown sugar

120 ml/½ cup organic sunflower oil

200 g/¾ cup Greek yoghurt

75 ml/⅓ cup coconut milk

5 UK large/US extra large eggs

60 g/¼ cup clear honey

2 teaspoons vanilla extract

225 g/1 cup mashed bananas,
super ripe (i.e. black)

Serves 12

Preheat the oven to 180°C (350°F) Gas 4. Oil a
30-x 17-cm/12-x 6½-in. loaf pan and line the bottom
with baking parchment.

Soak the dates in boiling water for about 12 minutes.

Mix all of the dry ingredients together. Mix the
wet ingredients together, except the bananas.

Drain the dates, remove the stones and chop
finely. Add the bananas and dates to the wet
ingredients. Mix the dry and wet ingredients
together until combined.

Spoon the mixture into the prepared pan
and bake for 40 minutes until golden. If
a skewer inserted into the loaf comes
out clean, it is done.

Cool on a wire rack, then serve.

Tunisian cake

45 g/⅓ cup polenta/cornmeal

200 g/1 cup golden caster/raw cane sugar

100 g/1 scant cup ground almonds

1½ teaspoons baking powder

215 ml/1 scant cup olive oil

4 eggs, lightly beaten

grated zest of 1 unwaxed orange

grated zest of 1 unwaxed lemon

2 tablespoons icing/confectioners' sugar

FOR THE SYRUP:

45 g/3½ tablespoons granulated sugar

freshly squeezed juice of ½ an orange

freshly squeezed juice of ½ a lemon

1 cinnamon stick

Serves 8

This particular cake is an all-time family favourite, and has always been received well. I love the fact that it can all be mixed together in one bowl.

Line a 21-cm/8-in. cake pan with baking parchment.

Mix the polenta/cornmeal, sugar, almonds and baking powder in a large bowl. Using a wooden spoon, beat in the oil, eggs and the orange and lemon zest. Pour into the prepared cake pan and put into a cold oven. Turn it on at 190°C (375°F) Gas 5. Bake for 35–40 minutes. Remove from the oven, cool for 5 minutes, then turn out onto a wire rack.

For the syrup, simmer the sugar and juices with the cinnamon stick for 5 minutes, stirring to dissolve the sugar, then remove the cinnamon stick.

Skewer the cake all over and pour the syrup over while the cake is cooling. Serve dusted with the icing/confectioners' sugar.

Antonia's award-winning chocolate fudge cake

Feather-light, rich, chocolatey, and award-winning. My little girl's great baking success.

175 g/1⅓ cups Italian '00' flour

2 tablespoons finest-quality unsweetened cocoa powder

1 teaspoon bicarbonate of/baking soda

2 teaspoons baking powder

140 g/¾ cup light brown sugar

2 tablespoons golden/light corn syrup

2 UK large/US extra large eggs

150 ml/⅔ cup organic sunflower oil

150 ml/⅔ cup buttermilk

2 teaspoons vanilla extract

100 g/3½ oz. dark/bittersweet chocolate, drops or chunks

125 g/1 stick unsalted butter

180 g/1¼ cups icing/confectioners' sugar

3 tablespoons finest-quality unsweetened cocoa powder

1 tablespoon milk

a handful of freeze-dried strawberry pieces

Serves 6–8

Preheat the oven to 180°C (350°F) Gas 4. Grease and line two 18-cm/7-in. cake pans with baking parchment.

Sift the flour, cocoa, bicarbonate of/baking soda and baking powder into a medium-sized bowl. Add the sugar and mix together well.

Make a reservoir in the centre of the flour and add the syrup, eggs, oil, buttermilk and vanilla extract. Beat with a hand-held electric mixer until smooth.

Spoon the mixture into the prepared cake pans and bake for 25–30 minutes. Cool before turning out onto a wire rack to cool completely.

Melt the chocolate in a heatproof bowl over a pan of hot water. Spoon the melted chocolate onto a piece of baking parchment and allow to set.

To make the filling, place the butter in a bowl and beat until soft, gradually adding the icing/confectioners' sugar, cocoa and milk to make a fluffy, spreadable icing.

When the chocolate has set, use the back of a knife to make curls with the chocolate to scatter over the top of the cake.

Sandwich the cake with half of the filling, using the other half to cover the top and the sides.

Scatter the chocolate curls and strawberry pieces on top.

200 ml/¾ cup whole milk

140 g /¾ cup golden caster/raw cane sugar

100 ml/½ cup double/heavy cream

5 UK large/US extra large egg yolks

160 ml/⅔ cup fruity olive oil

Serves 4–6

Olive oil ice cream

This original recipe comes from Giovanni Fassi at the Palazzo del Freddo in Rome. It will be devoured by even the fiercest sceptic. Serve with chocolate balsamic vinegar (see page 166).

Place the milk, sugar and cream in a pan and slowly bring to the boil. Make sure the sugar has dissolved. Remove from the heat and leave to cool.

Whisk the egg yolks in a bowl with a balloon whisk.

When the milk and cream mixture is cool, add the egg yolks, a little at a time, to the pan over a low heat. You are aiming to create a custard. When the egg and milk mixture has thickened enough to coat the back of a spoon, remove it from the heat. Add the oil and whisk the mixture with a balloon whisk until well incorporated.

Place in an ice-cream maker and churn according to the manufacturer's instructions. Alternatively, place it in a metal tin in the freezer. You will need to remove the metal tin from the freezer and whisk the ice cream every hour and a half until it is smooth.

Cook's note: This recipe can also be made with coconut milk instead of cow's milk.

Baked figs with hazelnuts and fromage frais

Italy's best figs come from the Naples area, having had all summer to ripen in the hot sun. Frangelico goes beautifully with figs, but you could use vermouth instead.

12 ripe fresh figs

115g/1 scant cup of shelled hazelnuts, toasted and halved

1 tablespoon mild clear honey

2 tablespoons balsamic vinegar

3 tablespoons Frangelico (hazelnut liqueur)

115 g/½ cup fromage frais/low-fat organic cream cheese

Serves 4

Preheat the oven to 200°C (400°F) Gas 6. Cut a tiny slice off the bottom of each fig so that it will sit stably. Make two cuts down through their tops, about 2.5 cm/1 in. deep, at right angles to one another. Ease each fig open, squeezing their middles to make the 'petals' open out a bit.

Mix most of the nuts with the honey, balsamic vinegar, Frangelico and fromage frais/cream cheese. Spoon this into the opened-out figs and arrange them in a baking dish.

Bake for 15 minutes until the cheese is bubbling. Sprinkle over the remaining toasted hazelnuts and serve.

Cocktails, marinades and infusions

Vinegar-based cocktails

Vinegar-based cocktails are currently a favourite on the London cocktail circuit and rightly so. The vinegar cuts through the sweetness of the cocktail, adding a delicious sweet and sour flavour. You'll have difficulty stopping at one glass!

Queen of tarts

A balsamic strawberry temptress.

1 part dry Martini
½ part Vodka
juice of ½ lemon
3 teaspoons caster/granulated sugar
3 teaspoons balsamic vinegar
6 strawberries, puréed

Serves 1

Combine all of the ingredients and serve over ice.

Mon chéri

For all those chocolate and cherry lovers!

1 part Grand Marnier
½ part rum
2 tablespoons finely grated dark/bittersweet chocolate
¼ part cherry liqueur
2 teaspoons cider vinegar

Serves 1

Shake all the ingredients together and serve with ice.

Herb vinegar

500 ml/2 cups red wine
500 ml/2 cups white wine vinegar
2–3 garlic cloves, peeled and cut
3 sprigs fresh thyme
3 sprigs fresh rosemary
3 sprigs fresh oregano
8–10 peppercorns, crushed

Makes
1 litre/4 cups

Occasionally we have some good red wine left over after dinner, and it really shouldn't be wasted. My Nonna was very frugal and was keen to teach the rest of the family to do the same. 'One day you will have a Ferrari if you are frugal enough!' she used to say. Here is a family recipe, which is a superb partner for the finest olive oil.

Mix the red and white wine vinegar together. Add all of the other ingredients. Pour it all into a bottle and seal. Put it away for at least 1 month. You will have the most deliciously flavoured wine vinegar.

Raspberry vinegar

500 g/4 scant cups raspberries
300 ml/1¼ cups cider vinegar
175 g/¾ cup sugar

Makes
500 ml/2 cups

Easy, stunning, versatile and so, so colourful. Please have a go. Make it for family and friends as a gift. Once you have tried it, you may like to try a gooseberry and lemon balm version.

Crush the berries with a fork in a large glass bowl and pour over the vinegar. Cover and leave for 4 days, stirring once or twice.

Carefully strain through muslin/cheesecloth (don't crush the fruit or the vinegar will turn cloudy). You should have approximately 500 ml/2 cups of liquid.

Boil the raspberry liquid with the sugar very gently until the sugar has dissolved. Pour it into warm, sterilized jars. The vinegar will keep for a year. Great news!

Chocolate balsamic vinegar

50 ml/3 tablespoons cider vinegar
50 ml/3 tablespoons balsamic vinegar
50 g/2 oz. dark/bittersweet chocolate (minimum 70 % cocoa solids), finely grated
75 g/scant ½ cup soft brown sugar

Makes
150ml/⅔ cup

Serve with ice cream, salads, and even steak. You will be surprised.

In a medium-sized saucepan, gently heat the vinegars and sugar. Stir until the sugar has dissolved. Slowly bring to the boil and allow to boil for 5 minutes. Remove the pan from the heat, whisk in the chocolate and leave to cool.

Decant into a sterilized jar when cold.

Easy marinades

The piri-piri marinade is perfect for chicken and will make enough to cover six chicken breasts. Likewise, the Japanese yakitori marinade goes very well with fish and will happily serve six. Use both marinades immediately.

Piri-piri marinade

Char 6 red chillies/chiles, then skin, deseed and blitz them in a food processor with 3 garlic cloves, 1 tablespoon chopped oregano, 4 tablespoons olive oil, 1 teaspoon smoked/Spanish paprika, 1 teaspoon red wine vinegar, sea salt and the juice and zest of 1 unwaxed lemon.

Japanese yakitori marinade

3 teaspoons caster/granulated sugar

4 tablespoons soy sauce (tamari is good)

4 tablespoons mirin rice wine

2 tablespoons sake

2 tablespoons groundnut oil

Mix all the above ingredients together and use immediately.

Folk medicine

Not only are they delicious, but oils and vinegars can even improve our health and help fight ailments, such as migraines, as well as more serious diseases like diabetes. My Nonna swore by brushing her teeth with extra virgin olive oil daily – wonderful for healthy gums and a bright, white smile.

Olive leaf infusion for diabetes

Roughly chop olive leaves until you have 2 tablespoons' worth. Place them in a saucepan. Add 1 litre/4 cups of cold water, cover and leave to macerate overnight. Next morning, heat the preparation slowly, and remove from the heat when it reaches boiling point. Leave to infuse for 20 minutes and then strain.

Drink the infusion in four separate draughts during the day – first thing in the morning, between main meals and before retiring. This linctus is full of absolutely vital antioxidants.

Migraines

Vinegar inhalations have been shown to be very helpful for this common complaint. Fill two-thirds of a receptacle with boiling water and add a full glass of vinegar.

Cover your head and shoulders with a thick towel and inhale the preparation for 15 minutes. Thoroughly dry your face and lie down for half an hour in a calm room.

Sources and suppliers

UK

THE OIL MERCHANT
www.oilmerchant.co.uk
A wide variety of olive oils from across Europe, South Africa and Lebanon as well as balsamic, wine, Sherry and flavoured vinegars.

SHEEPDROVE ORGANIC FARM
www.sheepdrove.com
A number of fine organic products including an extra virgin olive oil from their small olive grove at Can Toni Martina in Ibiza.

SCRUBBY OAK FINE FOODS
www.scrubbyoakfinefoods.co.uk
A hand-made selection of artisan English vinegars.

RACALIA SICILIAN OIL
www.racalia.com
Producer of high-quality olive oil and citrus fruits.

WAITROSE
www.waitrose.com
A wide range of olive oils and vinegars for keen cooks.

US

GUSTARE OILS & VINEGARS
www.gustareoliveoil.com
Extra virgin olive oils and balsamic vinegars from around the world.

OLIVELLE
olivelle.com
Olive oils, herb oils, nut and seed oils, citrus oils and balsamic, wine and infused vinegars.

AUTUMN HARVEST OIL COMPANY
www.autumnharvestoil.com
A family-owned business specializing in natural oils and vinegars.

OIL AND VINEGAR RICHMOND
richmond.oilandvinegarusa.com
Wide range of international foods and cooking products.

Picture credits

All food photography by Jan Baldwin apart from:

Page 10 *below left* De Agostini/Getty Images Page 10 *below right* De Agostini/Getty Images Page 10 *above* © Stefano Bianchetti/Corbis Page 11 © Thomas Hoepker/Magnum Photos Page 12 *below left* © Igor Golovnov/Alamy Page 12 *below right* Dorling Kindersley/Getty Images Page 12 *above* © Image Asset Management Ltd/Alamy Page 13 Universal Images Group/Getty Images Page 14 *left* sodapix sodapix/Getty Images Page 14 *centre left* WIN-Initiative/Getty Images Page 14 *centre right* Design Pics/Ken Welsh/Getty Images Page 14 *right* Dorling Kindersley/Getty Images Page 15 *below* E+/Getty Images Page 15 *above* © Yadid Levy/Robert Harding World Imagery/Corbis Pages 16–17 © Jacques Sierpinski/Hemis/Corbis Page 18 *left* © Sergio Azenha/Alamy Page 18 *right* © Florilegius/Alamy Page 19 *below left* © Sollina Images/Blend Images/Corbis Page 19 *centre left* © Michael Schinharl/the food passionates/Corbis Page 19 *right* © Vito Arcomano/Alamy Page 20 *below* © Simon Rawles/Alamy Page 20 *above left* © Majdi Fathi/Demotix/Corbis Page 20 *above right* © Hussain Abdel Jawwad/Demotix/Corbis Page 21 *below right* © ALAA BADARNEH/epa/Corbis Page 21 *above right* © Owen Franken/Corbis Page 22 *below* © Mick Rock/Cephas Page 22 *above* Werner Forman/Universal Images Group/Getty Images Page 23 *below left* Stefano Amantini/4Corners Page 23 *above left* © Duffas/photocuisine/Corbis Page 23 *below right* © Daniel H. Bailey/Alamy Page 23 *above right* © Susan Wright/Alamy Page 24 © Mick Rock/Cephas Page 25 Mitch Tobias/Getty Images Page 46 © nimu1956/istock

Index

Figures in *italics* refer to captions.

Acknowledgments

Without their culinary insight and input this book could not have been written. I love working as a team and this has all been possible with the expert guidance and assurances and support from: Julia Charles, Toni Kay, Leslie Harrington, Delphine Lawrance, Jan Baldwin, Emma Marsden, Anne Dolamore, Judy Ridgway and Eric Treuille.

Thanks to Sally Daniels for her utterly professional approach, speed, efficiency and the ability to decipher my scribbles. To Juliet and Peter Kindersley for sending me some of their outstanding oil from Ibiza, and answering my questions so diligently. Thanks to Will and Val at www.racalia.com for providing me so readily with information and generous help. Their oil is a credit to their dedication. Thanks to Robin and Debbie Slade at www.scrubbyoakfinefoods.co.uk in Norfolk for their inspiring collection of beautiful vinegars and their super chat! To Charles Carey (founder of www.theoilmerchant.co.uk), who continues his quest to source amazing oils, with such dedication and passion. Frances Jaine, who works with Charles, has been a godsend in helping me select the oils – a delicious task. Also, thanks to Gareth Miles for his work on the US oils.

Special thanks to my editor Nathan Joyce for his keen eye for detail – a name to look out for!

Finally, thanks to my friend Margaret Godfrey for her support and prayers.